Printed by: Lucid Raccoon info@LucidRaccoon.co.uk

Published by: Loch Ness Book Publishing, lochnessbooks@btinternet.com

Books in the series:
  Alexander Battan Grant – His Legacy
  Alexander Battan Grant – Fisherman, Musician & Fiddler of Note
  Two Highland Fiddlers + 2
  The Scottish Highlands Fiddle and Piping Heritage
  Pipe Major William Collie Ross

ISBN: 978-1-8383993-2-0

PREFACE

From historic anecdotal word of mouth passed down through several generations, and Parish records, it appears that Alexander Grant may have been descended from an illegitimate line of the Lairds of Grant. He was born at Battangorm croft in the Duthil area near Carrbridge in 1856. In 1887 he moved to Inverness where he set up a fishing tackle and rod manufacturing business. Subsequently, he went on to achieve fame as a champion fly casting fisherman, and additionally played a vital role in keeping alive in the Highlands the tradition of Strathspey playing as it had developed during the 18th century. Popularly known as "Battan", (his place of birth being Battangorm Croft, two miles from Carrbridge), he was a close friend of James Scott Skinner (1843 – 1927), the brilliant and colourful composer and exponent of Strathspey playing. Grant died in 1942 at Tomnahurich farm, then on the outskirts of Inverness in 1942, and situated at the base of the burial site of Tomnahurich Hill.

In 1903 he established the first Highland Strathspey and Reel Society, and with Donald Morison, of Morison Ironmongers in Beauly as his assistant leader – (the shop still exists in Beauly today and serves the same purpose). When Grant passed away in 1942 the Society was reformed after the second world war by Donald Riddell who had previously taken over from Donald Morison as assistant leader. Donald Riddell was an ex-pipe major in the Lovat Scouts, and on leaving the army devoted the rest of his life to teaching pupils and making violins – both skills taught to him by 'Battan' Grant.

It is said that Grant took his first violin lesson at the age of ten but refused to go back because the tone of the teacher's violin was so bad. Even allowing for some exaggeration, this story accurately reflects Grant's interest in the sound quality of the instrument – a subject which preoccupied him for most of his life. He probably made his first fiddles while still in his early twenties, although the earliest Grant fiddle known at the present time dates from 1886, when the maker was already thirty.

Throughout his life, Grant was never satisfied simply with copying the violin designs of Italian masters such as Stradivari or Guarneri and there are numerous examples of his experimenting with different designs on display in Inverness Museum and Art Gallery (IMAG), and in the store room. Most notably was the effort he put into designing and building both a round body fiddle and also a cello which he called a Rondello, and Roncello. He was convinced that the curved shape of a conventional violin and its internal features were an impediment to producing pure tones nearer to those of the human voice. However, he did not succeed in this quest in eliminating what he called 'the overtones' which the instruments produced at that time, and in the end had to concede that the Cremonese built models were the best.

Indeed, you may have wondered how the violin came to be the shape that it is. You will undoubtedly be astonished to learn that the exact shape off a Stradivari Violin, (or any of the other master builder's instruments of the time), can be re-created using Euclidian geometry. With just a straight edge, a pair of dividers, (no maths, just ratios and numbers), and the 'Golden Ratio'. This geometric technique, favoured by the great Master painters of the time, even modern day architects, and very evident on the finger board of guitars, presents a little known skill which apparently began with the famous family of Amati. (It has been said by some traditional fiddle players who have played the Grant fiddle in Morisons Ironmongers in Beauly that 'it sounds better than a Stradivarious' – however, you need to read the final chapter and make up your own mind).

Grant's crowning achievement in terms of achieving fame, (and also earning his primary source of income), was his patented design of the Grant Vibration fishing rod. This interest resulted in his invention of a unique design of fishing rod, based on principles which are closely allied to those of the fiddle – (a rod which was in big demand throughout the UK and parts of Europe for nearly 80 years). The rods were in two, three or four sections, usually made of green-heart wood, each section being joined to the other by overlapping splices, held in place by leather thonging. Because of the constant unperturbed vibrations of the wood throughout the rod, it was possible to cast enormous distances with little effort, and it was unknown for a rod in good condition to break. The invention took the angling world by storm, particularly after Grant achieved a world record cast of almost 55 yards at a competition held at Wimbeldon in 1896. Grant had patented his invention two years earlier, and at this time was making rods single-handed in his workshop in 1900, Baron Taylor Lane, Inverness. Eventually when he could no longer cope with the demand for them, he sold his patent to Messrs, Playfair of Aberdeen in exchange for the royalties. From this time on, his creative efforts were centred on improving the quality of his fiddles, a task which had first aroused his interest in the early 1880s.

This all came about when by 1887, Grant had opened a shop in Inverness as a fishing rod and tackle maker. He often fished the Ness on the 'free day' (every eight-day made available to towns folk), but sometimes broke his rod when casting for far out fish. Looking for a solution, it was the combination of his instrument making skills coupled to the need to find a solution to this problem that Grant recalled his discovery of the 'thread of vibration' when experimenting with the thickness of violin plates. It was from this that led him to develop an *acoustic method* for determining the taper of a fishing rod. The result was a rod which behaved like a newly cut sapling: flexible, almost unbreakable and every part springing in unison. At the same time, Grant patented a *lap joint* which was non-slipping and allowed the rod to bend (and twist) as if it were made from a SINGLE piece of wood. There are many people around today to whom mention of Grants 'Vibration' rod brings forth a nod of remembrance and smile for the man and his achievements.

To this day Grant's memorabilia are on permanent display in a dedicated cabinet in Inverness Museum and Art Gallery. The contents of his workshop were bequeathed to the museum.

CONTENTS

Preface

Alexander 'Battan' Grant

1856 – 1942

(Fisherman, Musician & Fiddler of Note)

(Photograph of an Alexander Grant fiddle, owned by Donald Fraser at Donald

Morisons, Ironmonger, Beauly – courtesy Laura Fraser)

Part 1

INTRODUCTION – an overview of his achievements

Alexander Grant

(Studio Portrait)

Alexander 'Battan' Grant

Alexander Battan Grant

(With his cap back to front as always)

Highland Fiddle Maker and Champion Fisherman

Alexander Grant was born in Battangorm, on Spey-side, in 1856 and played a vital role in keeping alive in the Highlands the tradition of Strathspey playing as it had developed during the 18th century. Popularly known as "Battan", because of his birth-place (Battangorm Croft, near Carrbridge), he was a close friend of James Scott Skinner (1843 – 1927), the brilliant and colourful composer and exponent of Strathspey playing. Grant died in Inverness in 1942.

It is said that Grant took his first violin lesson at the age of ten, but refused to go back because the tone of the teacher's violin was so bad. Even allowing for some exaggeration, this story accurately reflects Grant's interest in the sound quality of the instrument – a subject which preoccupied him for most of his life. He probably made his first fiddles while still in his early twenties, although the earliest Grant fiddle known at the present time dates from 1886, when the maker was already thirty.

Making a fiddle

Throughout his life, Grant was never satisfied simply with copying the violin designs of Italian masters such as Stradivari or Guarneri and there are numerous examples of his experimenting with different designs. A beautifully finished guitar-shaped instrument is in the Museum's collections, dated 1892 and probably based on a design of Stradivari dating from c.1726. The tone of the instrument, however, cannot compare with its looks. It is marked "No.1 Battangorm" and no other example of this design is known, indicating perhaps that Grant was dissatisfied with the resulting tone.

There are a number of significant departures particularly in the materials used by Grant to make his fiddles which reflect both his personality and local conditions. Normally, maple wood is used for the fiddle back, sides and neck, and pine or spruce for the front, but many of Grant's fiddles have bog-fir fronts – a wood which because of its immense age, possess better sound characteristics, but is harder to obtain. The fiddles made from this material have a particularly fine tone. Another violin in the Museum's collections bears the label, in Grant's handwriting: "Strad make – late 1600. Front restored and whole body re-balanced giving correct relationship, by Alex. Grant (Battan), Inverness 1900". Whether or not the instrument is a genuine Stradivari, clearly Grant believed it was, and was confident enough of his own ability to feel he could improve on the original by filling the f-holes slightly, and thinning down the front and back. The instrument as it is now certainly sounds superb.

The sound quality of any violin depends on a large number of complex and interacting variables, such as the relationship between the front and back, the thickness and type of wood used, the angle of arching, the volume of air inside, and the type and thickness of varnish applied to the finished instrument – among many other factors. Grant's genius lay in so regulating these critical factors that his fiddles were much praised in his own time, and are still played and valued today.

Each fiddle would have taken him about 150 hours to make, and consisted of either 81 or 82 parts, depending on whether the back was made in two halves, or as a single whole. Grant does not seem to have felt it essential to make all the parts of his instruments himself, as some makers like to do, for most of the pegs and finger boards on his existing fiddles are clearly purchased, and among his tools were found a considerable number of partly-finished, manufactured sides, fronts and backs, which Grant would subsequently have worked down to the desired thicknesses. He must have been an extremely methodical man, for the contents of his workshop which have been acquired by the Museum testify again and again to his neatness and tidiness: even the smallest items such as bridges, and sound posts have been sorted into individual tin boxes, which fit neatly within other boxes for storage. To make the fiddle, he used an inside mould, around which the sides of the fiddle were built up, glued and clamped together. Grant never seems to have had a fiddle-making workshop as such, preferring to work at home in an upstairs room, as he did for the majority of his active life at Tomnahurich farm house, Inverness. This room seems to have been something of a private place, into which even close friends were not allowed, Grant preferring to bring examples of his work, for example, downstairs to be looked at and discussed.

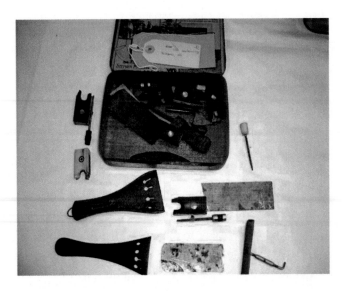

For Grant, fiddle-making was always a spare-time pursuit – although of over-riding importance to him – and never a means of earning a living. This he did in many ways, becoming a ploughman on leaving school, and thereafter shepherd, forester, gamekeeper, fisherman, grocer, hairdresser and fishing tackle merchant, before taking the tenancy of Tomnahurich Farm at the turn of the century. Grant's grandfather had been a woodturner and something of a clock maker, so it is perhaps not surprising that at the age of 18 he went to Cullen to learn forestry. This, however, he had to give up after a short time due to poor health, which plagued him for several years afterwards. However, throughout his life he had a passionate interest in what he called "the rhythmic or vibratory qualities of wood".

The Grant Vibration Rod

This interest resulted in his invention of a unique design of fishing rod, based on principles which are closely allied to those of the fiddle – a rod which is still widely used nearly 80 years later. The rods were in two, three or four sections, usually made of green-heart, each section being joined to the other by overlapping splices, held in place by leather thonging. Because of the constant vibrations of the wood throughout the rod, it was possible to cast enormous distances with little effort, and it is unknown for a rod in good condition to break. The invention took the angling world by storm, particularly after Grant achieved a world record cast of almost 55 yards at a competition held at Wimbeldon in 1896. Grant had patented his invention two years earlier, and at this time was making rods single-handed in his workshop above his hairdresser's shop at 4 Baron Taylor's Lane (now Street), Inverness. However, in 1900, when he could no longer cope with the demand for them, he sold his patent to Messrs, Playfair of Aberdeen. From this time on, his creative efforts were centred on improving the quality of his fiddles, a task which had first aroused his interest in the early 1880s.

In 1887, Alexander Grant opened a shop in Inverness as a fishing rod and tackle maker. He fished the Ness but sometimes broke his rod when casting for far out fish. Looking for a solution, Grant recalled his discovery of the 'thread of vibration' when experimenting with the thickness of violin plates. This led him to develop an *acoustic method* for determining the taper of a fishing rod. The result was a rod which behaved like a newly cut sapling: flexible, almost unbreakable and every part springing in unison.

At the same time, Grant patented a *lap joint* which was non-slipping and allowed the rod to bend (and twist) as if it were made from a SINGLE piece of wood.

Grant abhorred 'shooting the line'. Instead, he would pay out as much line as he needed then, using a *switch cast of his own devising*, loop it upstream and throw it out to wherever he wanted.

With upright eyes, Grant noticed that, at a point in the backward loop of his cast, slack line near the tip of the rod caused the line to loop back down the eyes. Tacking up this slack in the forward throw reduced the effectiveness of the cast. *Fall-down eyes* on the rod fixed the problem.

The Rondello

IMAG Display

Grant believed that the main shortcoming of the traditional fiddle shape lay in the fact that it had so many obstacles to the free vibration of the wood, such as the f-holes, and side bites (to allow for bowing), and that "while these exist no true tone can be produced. The tones you hear are simply over-tones blended, and not the full and true tones which can be produced on the new violin – tones nearer the human voice than can be produced on any other fiddle". The new "violin" to which he refers is his invention – the Rondello. This instrument, with its distinctive shape, is such a complete break with the traditional design as to justify Scott Skinner's description of him as "genius and inventor". The instrument is hollow throughout, including the neck, all braces and supports. Inside, a series of sound-posts, arranged in a circle around the perimeter of the sound hole, transfer the vibrations from the front of the instrument to the back. In the Rondello, each tiny part, including the distinctive bridge, has been designed and made by Grant himself.

The Highland Strathspey and Reel Society

Grant was the leader of the Society from its inception. It was founded in 1903 by a group of Inverness gentlemen with the aim of reviving "public interest in the old dance music of Scotland and of cultivating the art of playing this music on the fiddle". He continued as leader for almost 40 years, by which time he had become widely referred to as "The Scott Skinner of the Highlands". He also composed his own tunes, two of which are still played regularly by the Society, "Scott Skinners Welcome to Inverness", a march published in 1924, and "Donald Morison", a strathspey named after a Society member and assistant who was another close friend of Skinners.

Highland Strathspey and Reel Orchestra

Grant seated, 2nd left

Donald Morison was the owner of Morisons Ironmonger, Beauly. The shop still serves much the same purpose from when it was taken over by the current Donald Fraser's father. There is a small display of memorabilia, correspondence and a unique Alexander Battan Grant violin passed on to the Fraser family held in a small upstairs pitch pine panelled room. The photograph of this violin which has been used throughout this book was taken by Donald's daughter Laura. In addition to a portrait of Scott Skinner there is also Scott Skinner's will – displayed in a small frame hanging on the wall. The portrait is identical to that shown hanging in Grants living room in part 2 of this book – indeed it may be the same one.

The tradition represented by Alexander Grant was fortunately carried on by Society member, Donald Riddell, who became assistant leader under him in 1931, and who also learnt from him the art of fiddle making. His achievements and the legacy which he passed on are presented in parts 5 and 6. Post war, the leadership of the Society was taken on by Grant's pupil Donald Riddell Pipe Major in the Lovat Scouts, and crofter on the Lovat Estates.

Alexander 'Battan' Grant

1856 - 1942

(Fisherman, Musician & Fiddler of Note)

Part 2

BACKGROUND – a compilation of Grant's life history

Alexander Grant

(Studio Portrait)

Introduction

Alexander Grant was born in 1856 at Battangorm Croft (Battan becoming the name that he was most popularly known by), Carrbridge. He remained there for the following fifteen years of his life before moving to Garbole, Dalarossie, Upper Findhorn, with his brother Charles. Historical records indicate that the family had a long previous association with Battangorm with many relatives spread throughout the local area (Appendix 3). Alexander's father James [James died on the 18th February, 1892 at Battangorm] and his mother Marjory [Rose, Duthil] between them had twelve children of whom one infant was still born, Helen who died after seven days, Mary at 5 years, and two other sisters, Margaret and Ann who lived to the ages of 85 and 77 respectively.

Of his six brothers, James who married Margaret Calder [Gorbals] lived and worked locally with their ten children in Carrbridge with his occupation listed as butcher and shepherd. Charles married Isabella Darroch from Govan [two children], and lived in Kingussie working as a policeman and shepherd died aged 87 and having played the pipes. His brother David died in Petroria, South Africa, age about 33 years, of entric fever, was single and a Pipe Major in the Cameronians. Of his remaining three brothers, John, Peter and William all of whom at some time or another emigrated to, or worked in Australia. It was William however who featured in Alexander's life at a later date through an involvement in a financial investment scheme. The scheme did not make any profit business wise, and a further loss was incurred upon redeeming the shares upon the death of William due to the devaluation of the pound. William who was two years younger than Alexander remained single and died in his 70's. He is reputed to have invented a means of making paper from esparto grass, went to New Zealand then Australia and played the sock market. He part owned Edna May gold mine in Kalgoorlie and returned to Scotland to raise money in 1926/27. It would have been about this time that Alexander invested in one of his schemes. This is stated in one of Alexanders letters to his nephew (name unknown) and reproduced at the end of this chapter. On his death he left his fortune to his sister Margaret – listed as being a gold and water deviner! who was single, lived in Inverness and died age eighty five.

It was in 1886 having previously moved to Dalarossie with his brother Charles that Grant made a fiddle [his first?]. Following on from which in 1887 he announced his move to Inverness to start up business in Glenalbyn Building, Young Street, as a fishing tackle maker. By this stage of his life his skills with a fishing rod became apparent having the same year caught a 55lb salmon on the river Garry in September. His move to Inverness and his close proximity to the river Ness must have been for him a marriage made in heaven. He must have either been extremely gifted, or spent many hours practicing, or both, for him to realise the short commings of the rods that he was using. This subsequently led him to successfully patent his ideas and make a considerable sum of money from the eventual sale of his patent [Chapter 4]. The name 'Grant's Vibration Rod' is still in use today when anyone refers to his design of a Greenheart Fishing Rod.

In 1890 Grant began a long and close friendship with the renound fiddler James Scott Skinner. So much so that on marrying his wife Elizabeth (Bessie) Kennedy, Edinburgh [29th January 1891], he christened his first son James Scott Skinner [born 11th November 1891]. This in turn through his methodical habit of recording and storing information has led to the preservation of a considerable volume of correspondence from Skinner. Skinner unfortunately did not do likewise with the result that anyone researching J. S. Skinner [died 1927] would do well to consult the historical record of Alexander Grant.

At the outset of this book it was only the authors intention of researching the historical records of Alexander Grant. However, the closeness of Grant's association with Skinner has led to the inclusion of all of this one sided information flow as it relates to Grant [Chapter 3]. Furthermore, a lineage from Donald Riddell [Chapter 5], Donald Morison and his pupils creates a clear time line which ends with Riddell's pupils who are performing today, notably Duncan Chisholm, Sara-Jane Summers, and Bruce MacGregor [Chapter 6]. For this reason a very clear picture has emerged of the importance of Alexander Grant's influence on the Cultural Heritage of the Highlands which can be given prominence – the task now being to raise awareness and build upon these achievements for the benefit of today's and future generations of young musicians.

In 1892 Grant's deep interest in violin making and his determination to imporve its sound qualities was brought to light when he produced a guitar shaped fiddle. This instrument is today on view in Inverness Museum and is illustrated in the Introductory Section here, [Chapter 1]. However, his interests in the vibratory properties of wood also led him to imporove the durability and effectiveness of fishing rods – particularly those made from Green Hart wood. On the 28th May, 1894, he applied for a Patent (No. 10,385) relating to 'spliced joint for fishing rod' [Chapter 4]. His application was handled by Johnsons Patent Office, Glasgow. His application was accepted on the 4th May, 1895 and the Grant Vibration Rod was born. He had immediate success with his invention and his name and casting abilities with it became well known. So much so that he was invited to demonstrate his new rod's casting capabilities in December 10, 11, 12, 1896 to a select fishing audience at Kingston-on-Thames. Editors of "The Field" and "Land & Water" were present and he proceeded to out-cast all of his competitors. Further proof of his rods capabilities were noted with respect to the fact that Grant was not a big man, being of smallish light build and did not possess a large phyisical frame. In the passing of time others have claimed to beat his casting feat. However they have not achieved this useing his casting method - *so his record still stands to this day*.

In 1900, he sold his business in Baron Taylors Lane (fishing tackle maker, tin/coppersmith, hairdresser), and unable to meet the demand for his Vibration rod sold his splice patent to Charles Playfair, Aberdeen, for £100 pounds. (The name Playfair still trades to this day as a company supplying the highest class Premium sporting guns and rifles, and owner of Purdy – thee top class manufacturer of shot guns and rifles of various calibers which are sold throughout the world).

Battangorm Croft

Battangorm Croft - Marjory Grant, Sandy's mother, in

'Widows weeds' knitting a sock

Grant's mother died on the 5th October 1916 at Dalnansyde cottage, Carrbridge - his daughter Mary's house.

Sandy's mother in her late years

Part of the croft lands can still be seen between the railway line and the old road to Inverness. "battan" (or "baddan") means clump or small cluster; "gorm" means blue-green. The site of the house and steading lie slightly under the main road to the west of the burn but no remains are visible because the stones were taken away to build a house in Carrbridge (originally called Alderdale but, coincidentally, in the 1990s called Baddengorm).

The croft had a thatched, hipped roof and the 1881 and 1891 Census's confirm that it had 2 rooms and only 2 windows. The drawing (below) of a croft house was instantly recognised by Alexander Battan Grant's daughter, Madge Grant (1899 to 1996), who remembered the place from her youth. She confirmed that it had an earthen floor and that the peat fire never went out.

Battangorm was abandoned sometime after 1905. James (Marjory's/Jame's son), who ran a butcher's business initially from Battangorm [Mary, illegitimate daughter of Sandy Battan and Grand mother of Michael Kerr (78 at the time of writing - see later) could remember the awful task of cleaning out the insides of sheep in the burn]. He subsequently moved with his family to Carrbridge while his mother moved further up the burn to a wooden cottage reputedly bought for her by her son Sandy. The cottage, erected as a hospital when the railway was being built in the 1890s, (accidents when building the railways were not an uncommon occurrence) is today replaced by a modern house (although offset from the cottage site).

A house of the style of Battangorm

The above was instantly recognized as Battangorm by someone who knew it well. However, the proceeding photograph shows that Battangorm had a roof made of peat 'tiles' (not reeds as shown above), a chimney probably positioned nearer the end rather than the middle of the roof and a tiny, recessed porch. [Note from Michael Kerr – *Great Great Grandson of Sandy Battan* - 'we know the proceeding photograph is of Battangorm because: it came from a family source; it shows Marjory (Rose) Grant sitting outside the doorway and we know from other photographs what she looked like]. Battangorm had only 2 rooms and 2 windows (1891 Census) and was a logical development of the turf-sided house style of Strathspey. However, some drawings of the time are probably in error by showing a thatch of reeds because the photograph of Battangorm reveals that the thatch used in the Duthil area was, in fact, made of peat tiles.

Battangorm's all-stone walls were held together with mortar and the roof probably rested on the walls rather than on crucks. Inside, the floor was earthen and the roof space was open the length of the house (no ceiling). A peat fire, which never went out, warmed the whole house and helped preserve the roof. Carrbridge still has a good example of this type of house in nearby Bog Roy, but it now has harled walls and a red corrugated iron roof.

Side Note:

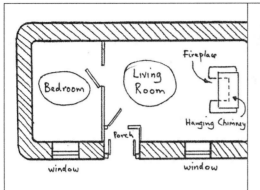

Likely layout of Battangorm

The hanging fireplace of a turf-sided house as shown in Highland Folk Ways by Isobel Grant.
Stone-built up to about 3 feet with a wooden canopy above to take the smoke out of the roof. Battangorm would have had such a fireplace but probably attached to the roof near one end of the living room.

Possible Connection with the Lairds of Grant (later the Seafields)

Background family history research carried out by Michael Kerr, great great grandson of Alexander 'Battan' Grant (see later), has uncovered an intreging link to the Lairds of Grant.

James Grant, Sandy Battan's father

In Michael Kerr's words:

It seems that we are descended, albeit via an illegitimate birth, from the Seafields. One James Grant [carpenter – not the one in the photograph], is probably the "natural" son of James Grant of Grant then living at Castle Grant and known as the "Good Sir James".

Note: "Natural" was the term used for the illigitimate offspring of the gentry; "born in fornication" was the term used for the peasantry.

What is the evidence for the connection?

1. There has always been a strong family rumour about it.
2. Marjory Grant (1899 – 1996), daughter of Alex Grant (Sandy "Battan") and grand daughter of James Grant [tailor – the one in the photograph], confirmed it (about 1989) without giving the connection except that "it was a long way back". The Seafield lawyer's were supposed to have approached Alex Grant about it at one time.
3. The Peoples Journal of 15th Mar, 1897, carried a very informative article of the life of Alex Grant (Sandy "Battan"), son of James Grant [tailor]. The story is so detailed that only Alex himself could have supplied the facts. The article hints at his lineage back

to the Laird of Grant in the oblique, reverential way Victorians reported any scandal involving the high born. (Whatever the gentry got up to was beyond reproach and put above the understanding of ordinary folk!)…"*Mr Grant is a native of Strathspey, being born in the Parish of Duthil, about one and a half miles from Carr Bridge….where his aged mother still resides, his forfathers having the right of clan descent granted them by the Chiefs of the Grants to abide there. Mr Grant's father (now deceased) used to remark his remembering when his father's holding [of Battangorm] was free. A moiety is now charged to establish the legal right of the proprietor, but the fact proves his family to have had honour with the chiefs of the clan in olden times.*"

4. Lady Caroline, who died in 1911, made special visits to Battangorm to see James Grant [tailor]. My grandmother (Alex Grant's illigitimate daughter Mary), who was brought up at Battangorm, can remember these visits [when other family members were asked to wait outside], which confirm that James Grant [tailor] was a "somebody". (The gentry were not given to calling on small crofters).

   "Natural" children and their descendants were "looked after" in case the legitimate family died out which in a way it did for the Seafields because, in 1881, Caroline inherited the Grant and Seafield estates from her only child, Ian Charles, when he died suddenly without issue. The barony of Grant became "extinct" because the title could only pass down the male line (the Seafield title, in contrast, could, and did, come down the female side).

   This may explain something my grandmother overheard James Grant [tailor] saying to Lady Caroline, "Naw, naw, Caroline, I hope it doesn't happen in my time." Lady Caroline was also supposed to have offered to build James a new house but his reply was, "Naw, Caroline, this'll do me fine."

5. My mother told me that, when she was in Austrailia in the early 1940's John and Peter, the oldest and youngest sons of James [tailor], both confirmed that Battangorm had been given to the family by the Grant estate.

How was it possible for an illegitimate son of the Laird of Grant to get connected with the Grants of Inschtomach/Battangorm? [Inschtomach – the ruins of this croft are still visible on the Foregin hill side, near Carrbridge, and is in the general area of where Battangorm croft was located].

Here is a plausible scenario, starting with a curious entry in the Inverallan (Grantown) parish records:

William Dunbar squarewright [a carpenter] in Grantown and his spouse Margaret had a child baptised (James) 14th April 1787 which was neglected to be registered by Mr Piery [name unclear] late schoolmaster of Cromdale.
Witness names:
James Grant, son to Sir James Grant of Grant,

James Seton, stocking weaver in Grantown.

[Sir James' son would have been about 11 years old at the time.]

"had a child baptised" is unusual wording for a baptismal entry in a parish register – there is no feeling of parental connection. Also, why was it "neglected" to be registered? And what was the Laird's son doing attending the baptism of an ordinary worker's son? Could it be that he was attending the baptism of his half brother under orders from the castle? If the child took his REAL father's surname and if he later took up the trade of his adopted father, then we have a good fit for James Grant [carpenter], {as detailed in an associated document produced by Michael Kerr – The Grants}. It would be natural for James Grant [carpenter], and therefore, itinerant to migrate from Grantown to Duthil where recent agricultural improvements were creating a demand for better buildings.

Caroline, Countess of Seafield
(On the untimely death in 1884 of her son, Ian Charles, 8th Earl of Seafield,
the Countess continued to administer the Seafield estates until 1912)

[Authors note: Michael, it has to be said, has produced a note worthy volume of investigative results on his family tree, giving precise detail of his forebears genealogy. His efforts stand out as a very well researched piece of work, worthy of any scolarly activity, See Appendix 3.

However, a further interesting observation from which Michael would not have consulted takes us to the correspondence addressed to Grant from Skinner (Part 3). In numerous letters to Grant, Skinner was in the habit of prefixing Grant's name with terminology such as: The Tomnahurich Genius; Genius of the Century; The Edison of the North; Brave Battan; and most intriguingly of all – 'Chief of Clan Grant'. It is likely that the mis-deeds of the Gentry would have been well known to the small community of Duthil (especially if a new offspring appeared and no one locally was known to have been pregnant!). Such stories would have been passed down and quite possibly Grant himself would have at some stage of their friendship have mentioned the possibility to Skinner – as above when he most likely gave the interview to the The Peoples Journal of 15th Mar, 1897].

Jim Grant (Sandy's eldest son) with cousin Willie Anderson

at railway hospital, Battangorm

Alexander Battan Grant

Sandy Grant (early 20's?)

"Sandy Battan" had a variety of occupations and no little fame throughout his lifetime. The Census of 1861 and 1871 finds him home at Battangorm. In the following years, Sandy tried his hand as an apprentice draper in Wales, a forester at Cullen (but had to quit due to a burst blood vessel in the lungs) and a grocer/butcher in Carrbridge. In 1881, he was a grocer at Garbole, Strathdearn (several miles up the Findhorn from Tomatin) and also did some hairdressing. Here he had a liaison with a local farmer's daughter and ended up getting her pregnant. The farmer thwarted marriage and forced Sandy to accept custody of the baby, a daughter, born 1883. He returned to Battangorm. By this time in his life, Sandy was an expert on fishing and fishing tackle so he tried large scale fly making in the winter and switched to being a ghillie in the fishing season (in most years for Lord Burton of Dochfour, Dochdarrach, Loch Ness). In 1887, Sandy removed from Carrbridge to Inverness, leaving his daughter, Mary, in the care of his parents. He started a fishing tackle business in Glenalbyn Building, Young St, but, as this brought insufficient income, he added hairdressing. About a year or two later he moved his premises to 7 Baron Taylor's Lane and, about 1892, he invented the Grant

Vibration rod, the consequences of which changed his life forever.

Alexander Battan Grant, 7 Baron Taylor Lane, Inverness

(standing, centre, in doorway)

Sandy's Great Great Grandson Michael Kerr

standing at the same spot, May 2019

(The shop is easily identifiable even today)

Having moved in 1906, his final occupation was as a farmer at Tomnahurich farm, which at the time before housing development encroachment lay just outside Inverness.

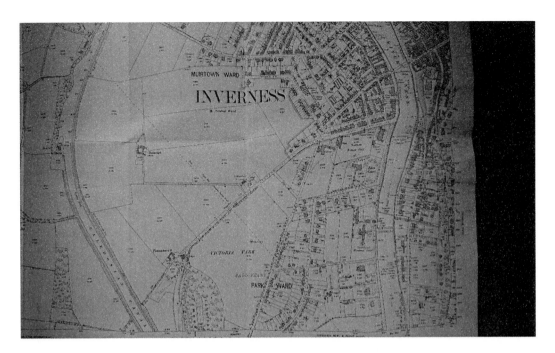

Tomnahurich Farm – bottom left near centre

His Legacy

Sandy's unique heritage derives from becoming well known in Scotland, the UK and abroad in two separate fields: fishing and music, in which for a man of his time, he made seminal contributions. He mastered for himself most of the skills he acquired, and the discoveries he made, in fishing and fiddling. Despite his unassuming nature, these achievements attracted the attention and admiration of the experts. In other words, his achievements could not be ignored by his peer group of knowledgeable people who were at the pinnacle of what was going on in both these fields.

His Main Achievements:

On fishing he was regarded as:

- An inventor of a fishing rod with almost magical casting capabilities and a

  skilled craftsman at actually making the rods. The Inverness museum has a

  collection of his rods (although they are not normally on display). Among

  other things, Sandy also invented the "Planet" cast, a simplification and a

  vast improvement of the Spey cast (and recently rediscovered!).

- A man whose practical and technical abilities in fishing were recognised as

  that of a master. Jock Scott, for example, wrote articles and the book

"Fine and Far Off", about his record casts and his complete skills as a fisherman. Sandy belongs to that small group of people who have caught a salmon of more than 50 pounds weight; and he once caught a salmon on the Ness at a recorded distance of 47 yards. With his all-round knowledge, experience and expertise in all departments, Sandy could well claim to be the most complete salmon fisher ever. [Sandy Battan's fishing achievements are detailed in Chapter 4].

On fiddle playing and violin making, he was regarded as:

- A very good violinist and a master player of Scottish music. His friend Scott Skinner recognised his ability in fiddle playing, particularly the bowing of Highland music. "Where did you learn to play like that?" Scott Skinner asked Sandy when they first met at a concert in Inverness (supposedly 1890), "Gie me your right hand and I'll gie you mine." In addition to being a top class solo player, Sandy led the Highland Strathspey and Reel Society, regarded as one of the best in Scotland, from its founding in 1903 to his death in 1942.

- A maker of violins of exceptionally neat workmanship and sweet tone. He obtained the good tone by tapping the plates and acoustically balancing them, i.e. making them, in some sense, acoustically identical. The Inverness museum has a display case featuring some of his fiddles, including a Rondello (a round disc shaped fiddle which was ultimately a failure).

Grant accompanied by Madge MacKenzie an ant of Michael Kerr

To help his rod and tackle business, Sandy became a well-known and ardent fisher of the Ness and worked fervently making rods. His invention of the Grant Vibration rod was driven by the need to reach distant fish on the river which, of course, is very wide. His achievement was to make a rod that behaved like a newly cut sapling before it dries out (he had noticed the difference as a boy). Many people think that the performance of the rod came from its lap joint, for which Sandy took out a patent (Patent No 10,385: applied for 28 May 1894, accepted 4 May 1895), but the real secret of the rod is its taper, which was worked out acoustically, rod by rod. The lap joint simply allowed the rod to behave as if it were made in one piece (other joint arrangements either don't bend and/or are points of weakness). It's no exaggeration to say that the Grant Vibration rod "blew away" the standards set by other fly rods and, in the late 1890s, it caused much controversy amongst the "experts" on fly casting (see the correspondence in the fishing and sporting magazines of the time).

Sandy Grant (2nd left)

Demonstration of the Grant Vibration rod on the River Ness,

below the Ness islands at the fishermen's shelter

Sandy initially made the rods himself in Baron Taylor's Lane, (now Street), Inverness, where he was also a barber. In 1900, he sold the design rights of the rod for £100 plus a royalty for every rod sold from 1900 to 1910 to John and Charles Robb of Playfairs, Aberdeen, who made the rods up until the arrival of modern rod making methods and materials (the 1960s?). As far as is known, Playfairs did not use the acoustic principle but simply copied the masters rods very accurately. Since the characteristics of greenheart is fairly consistent, a "copied" rod performs as well as a "real" one. While it was made, the Grant Vibration rod was 'THE' salmon fishing rod. Being the (near) perfect rod, it still performs better than modern rods but is much more expensive to make and heavier. The rod together with a tapered lined can be likened to a long, perfectly balanced bull whip.

The agreement for the sale of the rights to the rod is short:

Baron Taylor's Lane

20 Aug 1900

Inverness

Gents

I accept the sum of one hundred pounds Stg £100 for –

Firstly, My Patent No 10,385 viz. A non slipping splice for fishing rods

golf club handles and other like articles.

Secondly, My secret method of manufacture and wood treatment employed by me in the making of my vibration rod.

Thirdly, My registered ring used in connection with my vibration rod.

Fourthly, The sole right and power to make and sell my vibration rod.

Further I accept your undertaking to pay me a royalty of 10% on the net price of every vibration rod made and sold by your firm from 1st Sept 1900 until 1 Sept 1910.

All rods made by you to be numbered consecutively from No 1.

Yours faithfully

Alex Grant

After selling the rights, Sandy did not give up rod making. Correspondence with the Robbs shows that he helped Playfairs for many years afterwards, initially to get them up and running with the peculiarities of the rod but later to do specials or sort problems. In 1902, he built a workshop specifically for rod making but, unfortunately, it was completely destroyed by fire in May or June - only 3 weeks after its completion. Nothing was insured. (Michael Kerr – 'My grandmother told me that his sons, Jock and Willie, started the fire accidentally').

Correspondence makes clear that Sandy gave up active fishing for good about the time he sold the patent. He turned his mind to exploring the vibration principle in general and to its application to the violin in particular. Other pressures at the time might have been his founding, with others, of the Strathspey and Reel Society in 1903 and his take up of the tenancy of Tomnahurich farm in 1906.

Sandy was very disappointed with Playfairs' lackadaisical handling of the Vibration rod. He was particularly infuriated by the replacement of his fall down eyes with rigid upright eyes, and Playfairs' lack of drive in getting suitable tapered lines made for the rods (essential to its optimum performance). A quote from a draft letter to Charles Robb highlights his annoyance,

"Had you persisted in what I fought for single handed [in the 1890s] against all opposition in both art and execution, today there would be a different story to tell when you could rest on your own oars and pull as desired, [just] as I did and [be able to] laugh out all the Hardies in existence."

[In the 1890s, after the rod - and Sandy's prowess with it - hit the fishing world, a vociferous opposition, led by Hardie of fishing tackle fame, tried vainly to discredit him and the rod.]

Although brought up by a mother who was a very sincere Presbyterian, Sandy later became an avowed atheist and didn't hold back in trying to convert others (a brave thing to do in his day). [Michael Kerr – 'an uncle of mine told me what made him switch beliefs. Apparently, Sandy was struggling with the concept or an aspect of the vibration rod so he prayed and prayed to God for the answer. The solution to the problem came to him while he was cutting somebody's hair. He reckoned that he had worked it out for himself and that God had not bothered to answer him. I did not understand the story until I found out about the fervent religious atmosphere that existed in Duthil in the time of Sandy's youth ("Duthil Past and Present" by the Rev Donald Maclean published by James Thin, 1910). In those times, God was expected to answer your prayers in a very dramatic, vivid way - like writing on the wall'].

Sandy married Elizabeth Kennedy in 1892 in Edinburgh (a letter his brother wrote to him in 1897 confirms that Sandy knew her from his time in Strathdearn). She bore him 6 children, James, Ann, John and William at 4 Ardross Place and Marjory and Alexander in Rowan Bank, Ballifeary Road. His first daughter Mary came to stay with them in the mid 1890s and was there for the 1901 Census. His oldest son's middle names, "Scott Skinner", was in honour of the famous fiddler, now his new pal.

Elizabeth ("Bessie") Grant, nee Kennedy, Grants wife

Sandy Grant – the elderly Tomnahurich farmer

Letter from Alexander Grant to his nephew:

Inverness

12.12.35

My Dear Nephew,

You are a credit to all belonging to you and markedly to your Battangorm forefathers of whom you are a true descendant. But damit I can't get out of the multifarious position I am placed in and regret delay in answering your grand and eloquent letter of 27th July last. But my dear William it's not for the want of thinking about you and your kind and natural disposition.

Your token of a carved ivory fisherman with rod in hand is a present that will go down the ages! It is a marvellous work of art, one friend on seeing it remarked, "At last Battan's god's arrived!". Yes I replied, God was made by man and not man made by god!... You will be glad to hear – and not before time – it (my god) arrived safely. Your letter is remarkable in various ways, its terseness in elucidating the subject of rods, fishing, adverts and eggs for hatching from Blagdon Lake. This loch "Jock Scott" fishes year after year and kills trout up to 6 lb weight so that the spawn from it will serve you very well. Out there and receiving xxxxx from such a distance.

Your referring to Blagdon Lake and spawn from it induced me to send "Jock Scott" your letter. He published another book since you left for Hong Kong, "Greased Line Fishing for Salmon". Herewith his letter on sending me above book. He was very pleased to have got a reading of your letter which he returned and thoroughly agreed with you. He was north again this year seeing me. Before coming up here he was approached by a London Publisher to write a book comprising fishing done throughout the world wherever fishing is done – biggest bags on different waters, heaviest fish, longest recorded fly casting, rods and their principles and also the longest cast with fly in killing salmon. He wanted and walked to see the spot where I hooked and killed the salmon with 47 yards of line.

We all got a shock on hearing of your Uncle Willie's sudden death. I was put to a deal of trouble about it, but now off my hands having to employ a solicitor to certify deeds or other writings. He didn't expect such a sudden end and left his affairs in rather a mixed state, but one good thing his agent in W.A. knew him and probably most of his transactions for 30 years. Most of the letters received or copies were sent by Annie to your mother, who had written to you. A number of his relations and friends took shares in one of the mines he controlled, myself included and though we wished to get our shares returned at face value, it would be at a loss owing to the depreciation of the pound.

Now about the new fiddle. I'm afraid if not left from outside interference in which I'm involved and increasingly more than ever, as my nerves and energy are dwindling I may share the fate of your Uncle William and writing the great bugbear which I must elude. However, you will be glad to know I have one fiddle so far completed in detail with a resonance power and truth that it's tone should convince the most sceptical. But before proceeding with it alone, I must accompany it with a cello which can be more perfectly made or balanced (but a very stressful undertaking for me) owing to no counteractions as in the small instrument for holding under the chin. It will take celloist to their knees and never again touch their empty spurious tinpot noise boxes again.

I am writing this scribble on my knees sitting at the sooty fire in my recess where the remnants of articles made and unmade are jumbled together which you can hardly visualise!

With love to Mary and family – well and happy may they be, but don't forget a large (amount?) of my own best wishes on behalf of your noble self.

Your affectionate Uncle

Sandy.

I hope to be able to keep fit and see you all before I go.

Proof of Grant's everlasting contribution to:

The Cultural Legacy of the Highlands

(Grants memorabilia shown in the centre and right hand display panels at IMAG)

Grant's great great grandson Michael Kerr

(A violinist and instrument maker – May 2019, IMAG)

Examples of Grant's work

Michael holds one of Grant's Rondello's

Grant perceivered with the Rondello for most of his life but in the end

had to admit that the Italian model was best.

Grant's attempt at making a Roncello

(Quote from Grant - 'It will take celloist to their knees and never again

touch their empty spurious tinpot noise boxes again').

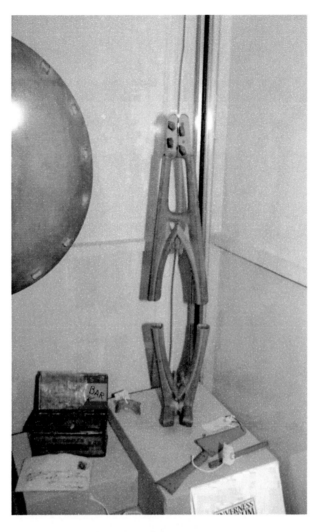

Frame for a Rondello and storage tin

Grant was meticulous in every thing he did. Small items were placed in tins which were then grouped in larger tins for storage. No one, not even his best friends, were ever allowed into his upstairs workshop. (An interesting voice recording of Donald Riddell telling this story exists on the Ambaile website - www.ambaile.org.uk).

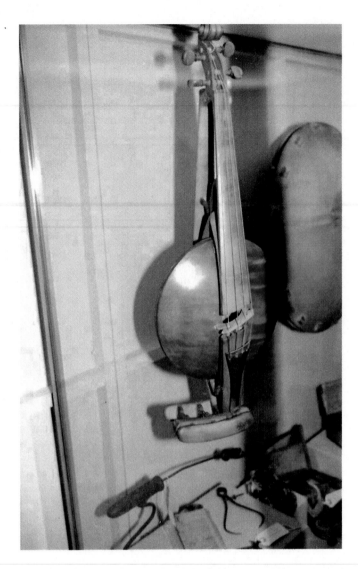

Grant made several Rondello's of which

a few are still in existence

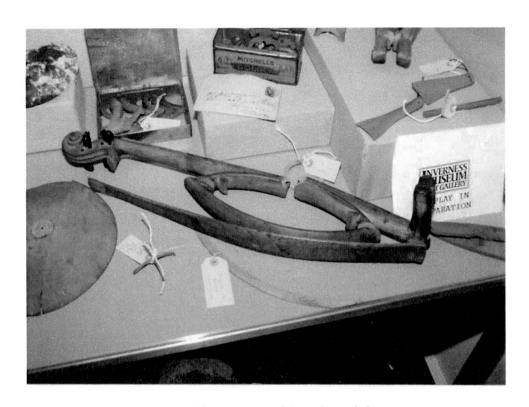

Some of the contents of Grant's workshop

which were bequeathed to the museum

The Music Tradition which he passed on.

STRATHSPEY & REEL ORCHESTRA. INVERNESS.

The Highland Strathspey and Reel Society in the 1920's

(Formed by Grant as its leader in 1903)

Standing: Mr Wheatley; _____; Mr Tom Gordon (Engine Driver); Mr Willie Mackay; Mr Duncan Grant (Watchmaker); Mr George Bell (Butcher); Mr Jim MacBean (Culcabock); Mr D.W. Call (Burgh Assessor for nearly 50 years). Sitting: Mr Alex Grant (Leader of the Society; Mr Duncan MacKenzie; Mr John Fraser; Mr Donald Riddell (became leader of the Society in 1973).

(Courtesy of Inverness Field Club – Old Inverness in Pictures)

A group at the Strathspey and Reel Dinner

Back Row: Mr William (Treasurer and Fire Master); Mr A. Duffie; Mr James MacKenzie; ____; Front Row: Mr Tom Macpherson; Mr John Fraser; Mr D.W. Call; Mr Alex Grant.

(Courtesy of Inverness Field Club – Old Inverness in Pictures)

Highland Strathspey & Reel Society 1935 – Alex Grant holding cap, Donald

Morison is in the front row, with glasses

(Courtesy of Inverness Field Club – Old Inverness in Pictures)

A tribute to Grant from the well respected Aberdeenshire fiddler J. Murdoch Henderson.

J Murdoch Henderson

(produced "Flowers of Scottish Melody")

"Battan, one of our most esteemed musical friends and well known to J.S.S. for more than half a century, was considered by the Strathspey King an "excellent violinist".

Battan's outstanding musical gifts are reflected in the solid, good work of the Highland Strathspey and Reel Society of which he has been leader and conductor since its inception in, 1903. "

Morisons Ironmongers Beauly

Donald Morison, the son of Roderick Morison, Ironmonger, Beauly was a local fiddle player of note. He had an excellent reputation as a fine fiddler, so much so that he became assistant leader of the Highland Strathspey and Reel Society under Grant, and also a close associate of James Scott Skinner.

One of Scott Skinner's best tunes has an indirect connection with Donald Morison. On one occasion, when Scott was Donald's guest, he was taken on a drive up Glen Strathglass to a famous and beautiful spot on the edge of the Beauly river. Sadly, this was the scene some time before of a serious road accident. A traction engine and two trucks had plunged off the road into a gorge and had killed two men, the damage to the wild birch trees growing on the banks of the river being clearly still visible. The sadness of the event moved Scott Skinner to write the tune titled *The Weeping Birches of Kilmorack*. Skinner later publish a tune in honour of his friend titled *Dr Morisons Seven Thistles* – still regularly played in a Gay Gordons reel set by Scottish dance bands to this day.

After the death of Scott Skinner in 1927, Donald set up a museum above the shop and displayed a number of items and artefact's – e.g. Skinners actual will and testament, hand written on a small piece of paper, still hangs in a pine panel room upstairs in the shop. In relatively recent times, a downstairs room in the shop also contained a collection of disused phonograph equipment which Morison had no longer found a use for, and, had superseded them with more up to date versions whilst still retaining the previous models. These unfortunately were discarded by a later owner of the shop, and probably contained the only sound recordings of Battan Grant that could have provided us with an unique opportunity to hear him play.

He was a man clearly deeply involved in his love of Highland fiddle music and must have greatly enjoyed the companionship of his two close friends, Grant and Skinner, when they came to visit and play tunes together.

Donald Morison suffered very badly from insomnia and had a cellar room, below the museum room where he played his violin, soundproofed, so that he could play at night without causing disturbance to his sleeping neighbours. It is also said that he was the first in the district to buy a bicycle with an electric dynamo in order to allow him to peddle about at night - thereby avoiding the pot holes in the road. Needless to say, Donald was quite unsympathetic towards any of his staff who had slept in and arrived late for work.

He was also said to be rather eccentric. Notes from the book 'The Village of Beauly', 2001, record that at the Kilmorack Parish Council meeting held on the 16th May, 1908, they elected Donald Morison, Ironmonger, to the Beauly Ward (7 seats). It must have indeed contributed to some lively discussions having an eccentric present.

Donald Morison with glasses on, front row,

with Sandy Battan on his right hand side

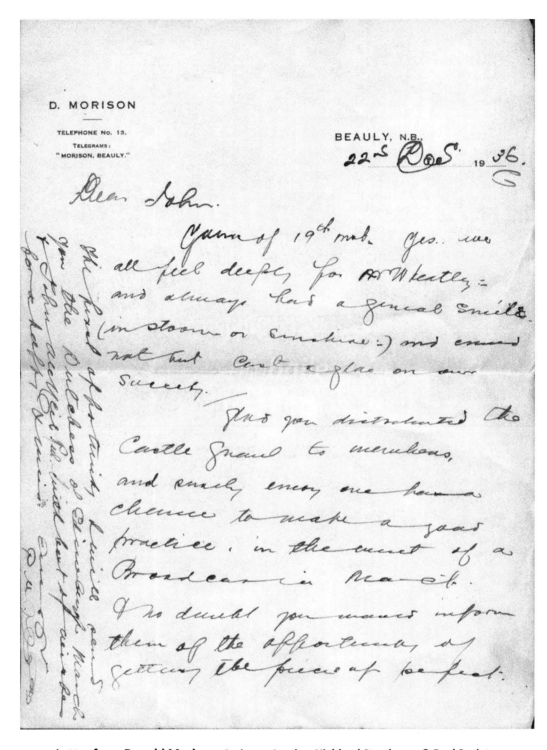

Letter from Donald Morison, Assistant Leader, Highland Strathspey & Reel Society.

In addition to concerts held in Inverness when Skinner was the invited guest artist, the three friends would have enjoyed many musical opportunities to play together in the down stairs sound proofed room in Morisons Ironmongers in Beauly. Their mutual respect for one another lives on in the tribute compositions of Grant and Skinner to their enduring friendship.

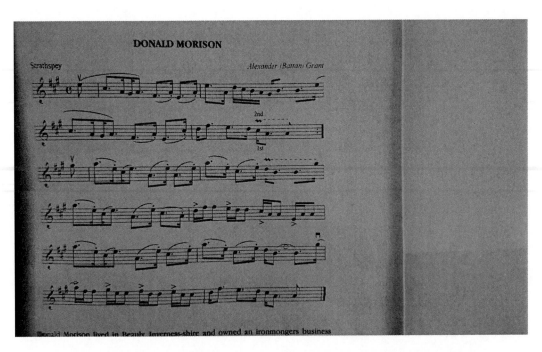

This tribute composition by Grant to his Strathspey and Reel Society assistant

leader Donald Morison remains to this day a popular piece

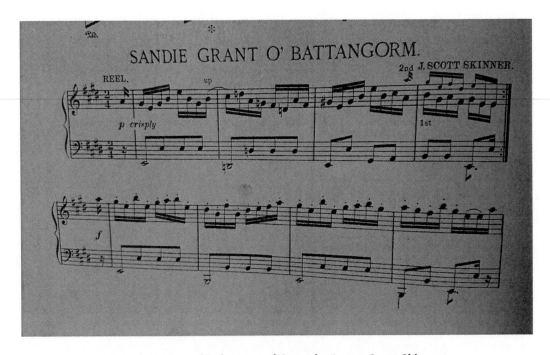

A reel composed in honour of Grant by James Scott Skinner

This composition by Grant was originally titled the 'King's Welcome

To Inverness' (meaning of course the strathspey king) is still

regularly played by the Society and Inverness Pipe Band

Compositions by Skinner honouring Grant

In 1973, Donald Riddell, who had been deputy leader before the war, reformed, and took personal charge of the Highland Strathspey and Reel Society. For the next 19 years until his death, he led the society with vigour and enthusiasm. His own fiddling talent, combined with his vast knowledge of traditional technique and his rare teaching ability, soon brought a wonderful quality and boldness to the Societies playing.

Donald Riddell who re-formed the Highland Strathspey and Reel

Society in the 1970's

Many of the young pupils he taught enjoyed much success at competitions throughout Scotland and went on to make a name for themselves as professional musicians.

The re-formed Inverness Highland Strathspey and Reel Society

under Donald Riddell – note the range of age groups

Donald had an interesting method for teaching young pupils. He would write out the tune to be played -right in front of the pupil – with all bowing carefully marked out. The pupil had the written music as a guide but learnt the tune by watching and listening to Donald carefully bowing it out. The pupil was expected to learn the tune by heart and play it correctly by the next lesson – otherwise no new tune.

Like his mentor, Alexander Grant, Donald restricted the Society's repertoire to a fixed number of sets, adding to the list only occasionally. Players became very familiar with the music and knew how to play it fluently. Years later, when members of the Society meet up, they unerringly play the 'old' tunes with exactly the same bowing and vigour as when they played under Donald's command.

Quote from Duncan Chisholm (Part 6) – "When I joined the Society there was a membership of approximately 30 members as I remember. These people varied in age from 10 years old to people in their 70's. There was a wide variety of styles and abilities within the Society but all were asked to play with the same bowing and in the same military style. As they played all were watched meticulously by Donald and although never directly pointed at, were made aware somehow that all was not right if the bowing they were playing was incorrect"

A Modern Tribute to Alexander Battan Grant

Held in Inverness 77 Years

after his Death

On the 14th June 2019

June 14th 2019

ACADEMY STREET
- INVERNESS -
Townscape Heritage Project

PRESS RELEASE

Traditional music session and talk to celebrate the work of Alexander "Battan" Grant

A free talk sharing the stories and music of Alexander "Battan" Grant, followed by a celebratory traditional music session, has been organised by the Inverness Townscape Heritage Project at MacGregor's Bar (at the junction of Academy Street and Church Street), 5-6pm, 14th June.

As part of its ongoing bid to create a greater understanding and appreciation of the history of Inverness, Inverness Townscape Heritage Project (ITHP) is hosting a talk entitled 'Stories and Music of Alexander Battan Grant'.

In the talk, Dr Sinclair Gair will bring to life the stories and music of Alexander "Battan" Grant, who was known for his superb fiddle playing and composing, as well as the design and construction of stringed instruments. A selection of his tools and artefacts from the Inverness Museum and Art Gallery will also be on display.

Speaking ahead of the event, Dr Sinclair Gair said: "Born in 1856, Alexander Grant was a British record holding distance fly casting champion; patented inventor of a new type of fishing rod 'The Grant Vibration Rod'; violin instrument maker and inventor of a new type of violin, the 'Rondello'. Grant worked methodically on everything he did, and I look forward to sharing details of his fascinating work. I hope to bring his work to life by also playing two of his compositions on the accordion - a strathspey *'Donald Morison'* and a march *'Scott Skinners Welcome to Inverness'* - followed by a move into the modern era of west coast style traditional playing."

The celebration of Grant's work will continue with a traditional music session with Bruce MacGregor, violin, and friends.

Musician and owner of MacGregor's Bar, Bruce MacGregor, said: "We're absolutely delighted to be hosting this event for this giant of the Scottish music world. My links to Alexander Grant are through the music taught to me by Donald Riddell who was a pupil of Grant. Donald often spoke about him and taught us the tunes and the style that Grant was such a stickler for.

"We have pictures of Grant and Riddell on our Highlander's Club wall of fame. So, this just ties it all in very nicely. It'll be great to hear more about Grant from Sinclair who has done a tremendous amount of research on the man."

The event takes place 5-6pm on 14th June at MacGregor's Bar, Academy Street, Inverness and is free to attend.

About the Inverness Townscape Heritage Project (ITHP)

The Townscape Heritage Project is a grant-giving scheme that helps communities to regenerate Conservation Areas displaying particular social or economic need.

Focusing on Academy Street, the Townscape Heritage Project involves funding from the National Lottery Heritage Fund, Historic Environment Scotland (HES) via the Inverness City Heritage Trust (ICHT) and The Highland Council, contributing to a project fund, from which grants are given to local property owners, businesses and organisations to allow them to carry out high-quality repairs and historic reinstatement to properties and spaces within the defined Townscape Heritage area.

The speaker: Sinclair Gair (Author)

Bruce Macgregor plays the Strathspey, 'Donald Morison', Comp. by Grant
(Some contents of Grants workshop shown in case)

The corner of Academy Street and Church Street (as it was in Grants time - just before the 1939 War). All of the buildings shown in this photograph have now gone (except for the church spire). The first building on the left in Academy Street is now the site of MacGregors Bar as shown below.

(Courtesy of Inverness Field Club – Old Inverness in Pictures)

MacGregors Bar taken on the evening of the tribute talk (14/06/2019)

(Forty people in attendance – house full)

Sandy Grant: A Personal History

The following was taken from a hand written account by Grant himself, found on the back of an old envelope.

I had to give up my forestry occupation and rest from manual labour for two years owing to a lacerated lung and the putting up of blood and went home to Battangorm in the Parish of Duthil. I was a bit of a fiddler and not satisfied with the fiddle I had nor others I tried. Having now the time, I started the – to me inspiring hobby of fiddle making. While pursuing my experiments and after making a number of different weights of thicknesses, I discovered what I understood to be a thread of vibration and found the fiddle to be a mere semi box with a boxy tone built on arbitrary lines and having no true scale on any part of the fingerboard. To proceed on different lines lay in obscurity [at this time] and the only thing left for me was the thread of vibration I discovered.

I was a keen angler from infancy fishing the Battangorm burns. When sound enough in health, I took a season's job as a fisherman to Sir [Michael] Arthur Bass (later Lord Burton) at Glen Quoich Forest. Going there year after year for four years in the fishing season and using my own make of rod, had the advantage and experience of seeing and using the guest's rods in comparison to my own. Some preferred their own and some mine but neither theirs nor my own provided what I felt should constitute the balance of a correct rod.

Eventually, I opened a shop in Inverness as a fishing rod and tackle maker. We had free days on the Ness every eight day and I was taking advantage of this like others and still experimenting how to make a correct rod. I got the mania for both angling and rod making which helped me in the rod and tackle business. This went on for 2 or 3 years, and scarcely a free day but I was coming home with a broken rod, not being able from an even effort to get an even result and, when forced to cast a long line, snap goes the rod. If, going out with the best rod I could make, no better result could be got, I made up my mind never to fish again unless I could make a correct rod.

After landing 2 salmon from the pool, I was fishing and casting again when snap goes the rod as usual. Two young fishing friends came along as I was leaving the pool and one of them said you are a "hell of a man". There is scarcely a free day but you are breaking your rod; if you had to pay for them, you would be more careful and satisfied with a shorter fishing line. I said: that may be so but you will never see me fishing again unless I can make a correct balanced rod. They said: we are using your rods and they are the best we ever handled. I was told [by them]: once a fisher always a fisher – and you will never make a better rod. I said: if not, that settles it – I will never fish again. The night before the free day they always came to me about the state of the water and the kind of flies to be used and always the same interrogation: was

I going to fish. And always the same reply: I'm further off from making a correct rod than ever so that they need not trouble any more about me going to fish.

The evening before the fourth free day I sat down and in a moment it occurred to me: what about the thread of vibration I discovered when fiddle experimenting and would it apply to fishing rod? And no sooner thought than there a way to make it, complete in itself power for weight. In comes my two fisher friends and one of them says we need not ask any more about you going to fish. I was greatly elevated and answered as easily as I could that I was not going to fish tomorrow but all being well I would be out on the next free day.

The Tomnahurich Grants, c.1913

(Sandy at Age 57 with all of his family)

Back: Willie, Annie, Jock; Middle: Sandy, Jim, Bessie

Front: Alec, Madge

Tomnahurich Farm c.1913

(standing: Madge, Alec & Sandy Grant)

Final image of Sandy standing outside his farm house

In the background, encroachment of 1930's housing development along what is now Bruce Gardens road towards Tomnahurich farm house. The spire of St Stephens church – the old High Church, is clearly visible, top left. Further housing development in the mid 1950' led to the obliteration of the farm.

Sandy suffered from ailments all his life. Of those we know about: 1875, a burst vein in his lung; 1908, scrotal rupture (left side), cured by a truss; 1935s, severe inflammation of the lower bowel; and, finally, chronic anaemia preceding death as a consequence of atrial fibrillation.

On 6th July 1942 Alexander Battan Grant, aged 86, passed away at the Northern Infirmary – a short walking distance from Tomnahurich farm. His wife Betsy passed on a short time later on the 2nd February 1943 age 76.

In.
LOVING MEMORY OF
ALEXANDER GRANT
TOMNAHURICH FARM, INVERNESS
DIED 6TH JULY 1942, AGED 86 YEARS
BELOVED HUSBAND OF
BETSY KENNEDY
DIED 2ND FEBRUARY 1943, AGED 76 YEARS
ALSO THEIR FAMILY
JAMES GRANT A.M.I.MECH.E. DIED 5TH APRIL 1970
ANN GRANT DIED 6TH NOVEMBER 1975
JOHN KENNEDY GRANT DIED 21ST MAY 1979
(INTERRED IN DORES CHURCHYARD)
WILLIAM ROSE GRANT DIED 20TH NOV. 1980
ALEXANDER GRANT DIED 11TH DEC. 1984

T 40
H-1
G 238
1 89

Alexander Battan Grant lies buried in Tomnahurich Cemetry, about 500 yards from the farm in which he lived for 36 years. His wife Betsy Kennedy lies with him in a four layer plot with the names of five of his six children on the grave stone. His daughter Marjory's name was added to the gravestone on her interment in 07/07/99. His son John Kennedy Grant is interred in Dores Churchyard.

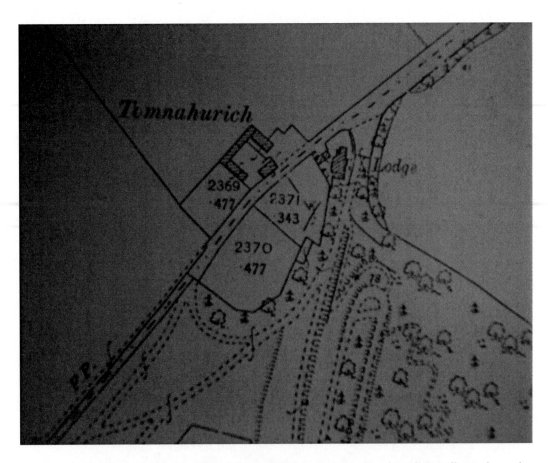

Tomnahurich Farm – showing the outline of the farm house and traditionally U-shaped

outer buildings arrangement.

(Lat: 57Deg 28Min 14" N, Long: 004Deg 14Min 37" W.)

Surveyed in 1866 & 67

Now the location of modern housing in Bruce Gardens

The Cemetery sits on and around Tomnahurich Hill (bottom right hand corner) which one see's when crossing the canal bridge going north on the A82 at the outskirts of Inverness. Grant's grave together with those of his family is to the right-hand side and just below the right walkway shown.

A Lasting Tribute

In life, Grant was described as being a wiry, slightly-built man, with finely-cut, weather-beaten features and penetrating blue-grey eyes, all surmounted by a shock of thick, tawny hair. Following the sale of his fishing tackle buisness in Baron Taylor Lane, Grant moved to Tomnahurich farm and started, at the age of fify, the lifestyle of an old-time farmer – a distinctly heavy occupation in those days. This would have become a way of life that was neither easy nor particularly lucrative – hence his music and fishing must have offered soothing comfort for the man. To those who new him he is described as a man possessed of an energy peculiar to himself which he was able to transmit – and transmit he did, because here, seventy seven years after his death, and one hundred and sixty three years after his birth, people such as myself find great interest in the man, and a desire to keep his memory alive and known to the general public in oder to celebrate his achievements and contribution to Highland cultural life.

His Motto and Driving Infuence in Life:

"Either a thing is right or it isn't, and if it isn't, it's not worth troubling about". Similarly, "Why" he said, "take any trouble at all unless you are going to take enough? An imperfect job is no use to anyone".

Chronological Time Line:

ALEXANDER GRANT (Sandy Battan)   Rev 5, 09-05-91

1856 Born 2 Sept at Battangorm croft, CarrBridge. Battan-gorm means clump/thicket of blue.

1861 Census (8 Apr): living at Battangorm (age 4).
: Left school (which overlooked Battangorm croft), (age 8).
: Supposedly refused fiddle lessons from a neighbour (the school teacher?) because he didn't like the tone of his fiddle.
:Herdsman and ploughman at Battangorm. (With no fences in those days, herding was necessary to keep the cattle off the crops.), (age 8/14).

1870/71 12 months as a hill shepherd at Cromdale.

1871 Census (3 April): reports Alex living at Battangorm (age 14).

1871 Apprentice draper in Wales for 2-1/2 years (age 15/17).

1874 Went to Cullen to learn forestry but later gave up due to ill health (burst blood vessel in lungs). (age 18).

1876 Started 2 years enforced idleness under medical stricture. (age 20).

1878/80 Started a grocer/butcher shop in Carrbridge.
: After 18 months, he moved to Strathdearn where shop keeping offered better prospects. (age 22).

1881 Census (4 Apr): grocer at Garbole, Dalarossie, Upper Findhorn with brother Charles. Also does hair dressing. (age 24).

1882 Romance with Catherine McBain, farmer's daughter, Corrievorrie, Dalarossie.

1883 Daughter (illegitimate) Mary McBain born 20 March at Morile, Tomatin. (age 26).

1884 Daughter Mary baptised at Moy 6th January. Sandy was present but no evidence that Catherine McBain was. About this time, Mary was handed over for care to Sandy's Mother in Battangorm. Also, about this time, Sandy returns to Carrbridge where he starts large scale fly making but without, it seems, managing to make a sufficient living off it. (age 27).

1885 Takes a season as a fisherman to Lord Burton at Glenquoich Forest (up the river Garry, West of the Great Glen), (age 28).
Catherine McBain, whom Sandy was thwarted from marrying, accepts her father's choice, Alex Tulloch, a worker on the Corrievorrie farm.

1886 Made a fiddle (the first?). His interest in the technicalities of the violin date from his time in Strathdearn.

1886 Takes another season at Glenquoich. Later takes a position, for a short while, as a gamekeeper on another estate.

1887 Announces (24 May) move from C. Bridge to Inverness and start a shop in Glenalbyn Building, Young St, as a fishing tackle maker. Capital shortage compels him to look for extra income so he adds hairdressing to the business and hires a barber. (age 30).

1887 Further to help income, Sandy takes another season at Glenquoich. He catches a 55 lb salmon on the river Garry in September, at the outlet to Loch Quoich. (age 31).

1887/88 Discharges the barber and does the hairdressing himself as well as make fishing tackle. Leaves Young Street to take up premises at 7 Baron Taylor' Lane, now Street.

1890 Befriends Scott Skinner who admires his bowing technique. (age 33/34).

1891 Marries 29 Jan, Edinburgh, Elizabeth (Bessie) Kennedy. Address given as Baron Taylors Lane, Inverness; occupation: fishing tackle maker. (age 34).

1891 Son James Scott Skinner born 11 Nov at 4 Ardross Place, Inverness. Occupation: fishing tackle maker. (age 35).

1892 Father dies 18 Feb at Battangorm.

1892 Made guitar shaped fiddle ("No 1 Battangorm"). At this time he is putting his discoveries on the acoustic properties of wood to practical use in both violins and fishing rods.

1892 First mention in a sporting paper of the Vibration Rod (Rod & Gun Sept 3rd). This was probably due to R H Carballis of Moniack castle, a JP in Inverness, who had good contacts in the fishing world. He strongly supported Sandy in the disputes later in the 90's over casting competitions.

1893 First mention on the 7th April, 1893, in Land and Water, of the use of fall-down rings on the rod. (age 36).

1893 Daughter Ann born 27 April at 4 Ardross Place. Occupation: fishing tackle maker.

1894 Applies 28 May for patent (spliced joint for fishing rod). Patent No 10,385 of 1894 (handled by Johnsons Patent Office, Glasgow). (age 37).

1895 Son John Kennedy born 16 Feb at 4 Ardross Place. Occupation: fishing tackle maker. (age 38).

1895 Splice patent accepted 4 May. (age 40).

1896 Son, William Rose, born 6th Nov. at Ardross Place

1896 Demonstrates fly casting, Dec 10, 11, 12, to select fishing audience at Kingston-on-Thames. Opposite the Sun Hotel. Editors of "The Field", "The Fishing Gazette", "Rod and Gun", and "Land and Water" and other notables (including R H Corballis).

1899 Daughter Marjory born 7 Jul at Rowan Bank, Ballifeary Rd. (age 42).

1900 Sale of patent rights of the vibration rod to Charles Playfair, Aberdeen, for £100 plus %10 royalty per rod for 10 years. Rods to be numbered consecutively from 1. (age 45/46).

1900 Approx. date for sale of business in Baron Taylors Lane (fishing tackle maker, tin/coppersmith, hairdresser).

1901 Brother David, pipe major of the Cameron Highlanders, dies in S. Africa.

1902 Son Alexander born 26 Nov at Ballifeary Rd. (age 48).

1903 Daughter Mary marries 10 Apr at Battangorm from 4 Hill St, Inverness. Sandy's occupation given as hairdresser.

1903 Founds Highland Strathspey and Reel Society and leads it for the rest of his lifetime. (age 48).

1906 Moves to Tomnahurich farm, Inverness.

1916 Mother dies 5 Oct at Dalnansyde cottage, Carr Bridge (daughter Mary's house).

1924 Publishes "Scott Skinner's Welcome to Inverness".

1927 Scott Skinner dies.

1934 or 35 Radio broadcast of Highland Strathspey and Reel Society.

1942 Dies 6 July, aged 85.

1943 Wife Bessie dies 2 Feb, age 76.

Date unknown: caught 8 lb salmon on Ness at distance of approx. 47 yards.

A local poet, Bernard George Hoare, wrote the following lines in Grant's memory:

Master of violins and of the bow

That sweeps the strings to tuneful melody,

Player of lively airs and tunes that be

The genius of your native Strath's outflow,

With kindred genius nature did bestow

On you the finer sense of music's round

And perfect tone; the laws of sound

Enthralled you, as her child to trace and know.

Craftsman and builder of a truer tone

Than even the violin now can, mastered charm;

Who seeks for perfect finds it not alone,

Since in the seeking also lies the form.

You are the silent poet, tuning all the strings

To perfect interval, where false still rings.

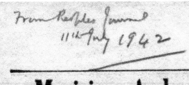

*From Peoples Journal
11th July 1942*

Musician And Inventor

Death Of Notable Highlander

LOVERS of Highland music not only in this country but abroad will mourn the death of Mr Alexander Grant, Tomnahurich Farm, Inverness, for, a brilliant fiddler, he was one of the greatest exponents of this type of music since that other noted player, Scott Skinner.

Mr Grant, who died in the Royal Northern Infirmary on Monday after a lingering illness, devoted most part of his life to the propagation of the characteristic music of the Highlands, marches, strathspeys, and reels.

Born at Battan Gorm, near Carr Bridge, 86 years ago, Mr Grant began at the early age of 10 what turned out to be a truly remarkably brilliant career as a violinist. Even then he showed a keen sense of the true quality of music, for it is recalled by his friends that when his father sent him to a neighbour to learn to play he refused to go again because the tone of the teacher's fiddle was bad.

The Master Touch.

Principally by self-tuition Mr Grant gradually acquired the master touch, and he became such a brilliant player that he was generally regarded as being the "Scott Skinner of the Highlands."

Mr Grant had a varied and interesting career. After leaving school he was in turn a ploughman, shepherd, draper, forester, grocer, butcher, gamekeeper, fisherman, and fishing tackle merchant in Inverness.

He became tenant of Tomnahurich Farm about 40 years ago, and it was from that time that he really began to develop his very great interest in Highland music.

He accomplished much good work as leader of the Highland Strathspey and Reel Society. It was with the aim of improving the playing of marches, strathspeys, and reels that he helped to form this society some 40 years ago, and he gave it his inspired leadership from its inception until a short time ago.

As leader of the society, Mr Grant was extremely popular, not only with members but with the public. The latter delighted to see the veteran wielding the baton, and gave him a rousing reception, particularly at the time-honoured wool fair concerts given by the society round about this period of the year.

Born Genius.

"Battan," the name by which he was known to all his friends, composed several pieces of Highland music, including the march, "Scott Skinner's Welcome," and the strathspey and reel, "Donald Morison," the last-mentioned being a musical tribute to one of his oldest friends.

He was recognised by many as being a born genius with an inventive trait. He made several types of fiddles and for many years, up until his last illness, he was engaged on constructing a violin based on the vibration principle.

He claimed that this violin, which was unlike in design any other type, would, when completed, produce a tone so rich in quality and expression that it would resemble as near as possible the human voice. Unfortunately, Mr Grant did not succeed in his ambition to complete this unique violin.

Perhaps his most interesting invention was that of the Grant vibration fishing rod, which was regarded as being one of the best rods ever constructed. This invention created considerable interest amongst anglers, and Mr Grant was challenged twice to show its capabilities. Its worth was fully proved when Mr Grant, before a large crowd of anglers on the Thames, set up a record cast of 56 yards with a 21-foot rod.

Later from a boat on the River Ness he cast a distance of 65 yards with a 21-foot rod and 61 yards with an 18-foot rod.

The death of this interesting personality marks the passing of one who was popular with all who had the pleasure of his acquaintance.

He is survived by Mrs Grant and a grown-up family of four sons and two daughters.

This tribute to Alexander Grant, 'Musician and Inventor', is from the 'People's Journal', 11th July, 1942. The 'People's Journal' was one of many popular weekly papers which appeared in Scotland following the repeal of the Stamp Duties in the 1850s. From its inception in Dundee in 1858, it quickly grew into thirteen editions covering Scotland's major cities, towns and regions.

GIFTED VIOLINIST AND ANGLER

Late Mr Alexander Grant

One of the most remarkable and outstanding personalities in the North, Mr Alexander Grant, of Tomnahurich Farm, Inverness, passed away peacefully on Monday in his 87th year.

Mr Grant was a violinist of repute and was famous for his splendid rendering of Strathspeys and reels in the traditional Highland style. The late Mr Scott Skinner acknowledged that Mr Grant excelled him in bowing as well as in the playing of the older Scotch airs. To him Scott Skinner composed and published a reel named "Sandy Grant's reel." He was the leader of Inverness Strathspey and Reel Society from its inception.

Mr Grant was also an expert angler, and held the record for long line casting not only on the Ness but on the Thames.

A native of Strathspey, he, when a young man became head fisherman to the late Rt. Hon Lord Burton, lessee of the famous deerforest of Glenquoich, where he met many of the angling sportsmen of that day; to mention but two, Lord Randolph Churchill father of the present Premier, and Joe Chamberlain father of the late Premier, Neville Chamberlain.

In later years he opened up a combined hairdressing and fishing tackle maker's establishment in Inverness. He made violins on the model of the Cremona as a hobby. In order to do this he took up the study of sound-vibration which he mastered to a wonderful degree. The nature of the varnish with which the makers of the "Stradivarius and the Cremona" violins were coated was more or less unknown to modern violin makers. Mr Grant got busy, and if he came short of discovering the secret, he nevertheless succeeded in making varnish which was equally effective in coating the violin without in any way, (unlike the spirit varnish) affecting the tone of the instrument.

When applying his knowledge of sound vibration to the making of his violins it occurred to him that it would be possible to make a fishing rod in such manner as to ensure an uninterrupted flow of vibration along the fibre of the rod from butt to point and thus make the rod more pliant.

Famous Fishing Rod

In this he succeeded and turned out the best and most famous rod that was ever placed on the market. He ultimately secured a patent for it, and later sold the right to Playfair, Fishing Tackle makers, Aberdeen.

Soon the fame of the "Grant Vibration Rod" spread far and wide. This was naturally the cause of some resentment by many other good makers of rods, and in a short time all the leading sporting papers throughout England and Scotland were aflame with bitter controversy relative to the merits and demerits of the rod's casting capacity. In the end a challenge to a competition was issued to Mr Grant, and his supporters. The challenge was readily accepted and Mr Grant went to London, and in the presence of the best anglers and tackle-makers of that day, proved the superior casting capacity of his rod on the Thames without difficulty.

Within recent years, Mr Grant, not wholly satisfied that the tone produced by the violin in its present form was what it might be, made one himself on the most unorthodox lines. His view was to conserve the sound-vibration which in the case of the present model, he thought was dissipated by the "S" sound-holes. Whether he attained this end must needs be left for the expert to say, but that he produced a violin of the rarest beauty of tone, both sweet and mellow, cannot be gainsaid. The construction of it was kept secret from all but a few of his most intimate friends as he had intended to secure a patent for it. It is to be hoped that some day the patent will be secured and the new violin will become as famous as the "Vibration Rod."

A more kindly or unassuming person could not well be met with than Mr Alexander Grant. Many friends throughout the Highlands will regret his passing while this mention of his name must bring to their memories the rich feast of Highland music with which he entertained them at Woolfair Concerts of other days in Inverness.
                                                    J.T.H.

This tribute to Alexander Grant, 'Gifted Violinist and Angler', is from 'The Football Times', 11th July 1942.

Alexander Battan Grant – His Historical Archive

Sandy Grant (1890's ?)

Family photograph with Grant (2nd left), and presumeably – his wife

Betsy (centre), two of his 4 sons, and his two daughters Ann and Marjory.

At home with family – Grant 2nd right with his wife Betsy on his R.H.S.

Grant on the right with two friends

(probably taken at the same time as the Sudio portraite)

Grant with his eldest son James

Alexander Grant (1856 - 1942) was a native of Battangorm, Carrbridge, which gave rise to his familiar name - 'Battan'. As a boy he was exposed to what were to become his two great passions - fiddling and fishing. He went on to excel in both areas; as an angler by inventing his own unique fishing rod known as the 'Grant Vibration Rod', and as a fiddler by leading the Highland Strathspey and Reel Society for almost forty years and by becoming an expert in fiddle making techniques. He also invented a unique disc-shaped violin known as a 'Rondello'. An example of Grant's fishing rod, fiddle and Rondello can be seen at Inverness Museum and Art Gallery (IMAG).

This photograph shows an elderly Alexander Grant (centre) at home with his daughter and friends, one of whom is holding a Grant 'Vibration' fishing rod.

Alexander Grant (1856 - 1942) was a native of Battangorm, Carrbridge, which gave rise to his familiar name - 'Battan'. As a boy he was exposed to what were to become his two great passions - fiddling and fishing. He went on to excel in both areas; as an angler by inventing his own unique fishing rod known as the 'Grant Vibration Rod', and as a fiddler by leading the Highland Strathspey and Reel Society for almost forty years and by becoming an expert in fiddle making techniques. He also invented a unique disc-shaped violin known as a 'Rondello'. An example of Grant's fishing rod, fiddle and Rondello can be seen at Inverness Museum and Art Gallery (IMAG).

In May 1887 Grant moved his fishing rod and tackle business from Carrbridge to Inverness, initially at Glenalbyn Buildings, Young Street. He later moved to premises at 7 Baron Taylor's Lane. This photograph shows Grant's business premises in Baron Taylor's Lane which incorporated a tin and coppersmith, a haircutting and shaving saloon, and the fishing rod and tackle business. The gentleman standing outside the front door (centre) may be Mr. Grant in his earlier years.

Tomnahurich translates as 'the hill of the yew trees' and is also known as the 'Fairy Hill'. The 16th or 17th century prophet, the Brahan Seer, predicted the coming of the Caledonian Canal - "full-rigged ships will be seen sailing eastward and westward by the back of Tomnahurich. The area was also the scene of an annual horse race from the 17th century.

The Scottish Clans' Association
(of LONDON).

Association's Head Quarters:
ROYAL SCOTTISH CORPORATION HALL,
Fleet Street, E.C.
(Entrance, Crane Court.)

Chief.
Dr. W. AITKIN MAC LEOD.

Hon. President.
Gen. Sir HECTOR A. MACDONALD, K.C.B.,
D.S.O., A.D.C.

President.
DONALD N. NICOL, Esq., M.P.

Vice-Presidents.
Sir ROBERT B. FINLAY, K.C., M.P., Attorney-General.
Sir WILLIAM JOHNSTON, Bart.
ROBERT CAMERON, Esq., M.P.
JAMES MEAD SUTHERLAND, Esq.
A. C. MACKENZIE, Esq.
JAMES WATSON, Esq.   JAMES BUCHANAN, Esq.
JOHN ROEBUCK, Esq.   GEORGE ROSS, Esq.
GILMOUR ORR, Esq.   Lieut. NEIL MACKAY.
Lieut. E. S. GRAHAM, R.G.A.

Hon. Auditor—
Mr. ANGUS N. SCOTT, C.A.,
18, Ironmonger Lane, E.C.

Bankers—
Messrs. CHILD & Co.,
1, Fleet Street, E.C.

Hon. Treasurer:
GEO. C. WALLACE,
227, Regent Street, W.

Hon. Secretary:
WILLIAM MACKENZIE FRASER,
26, Portland Road,
Holland Park, W.

Hon. Assistant Secretary:
JOHN MACINTYRE MASSON,
16, Rutland Park Mansions,
Willesden Green, N.W.

PATRONS.

His Grace the Duke of Richmond and Gordon, K.G., P.C.
His Grace the Duke of Hamilton.
His Grace the Duke of Montrose, K.T.
His Grace the Duke of Buccleuch & Queensberry, K.G., K.T.
His Grace the Duke of Argyll, K.T., G.C.M.G., P.C.
The Most Hon. the Marquess of Huntly, P.C.
The Most Hon. the Marquess of Breadalbane, K.G., P.C.
The Right Hon. the Earl of Haddington.
The Rt. Hon. the Earl of Kinnoull.

The Rt. Hon. the Earl of Dundonald, C.B., M.V.O
The Rt. Hon. Earl of Kintore, G.C.M.G., P.C.
The Rt. Hon. Lord Abinger.
The Rt. Hon. Lord Stratheden and Campbell.
The Rt. Hon. Lord Blythswood.
The Rt. Hon. Lord Kinnaird.
The Rt. Hon. A. J. Balfour, M.P., P.C.
The Rt. Hon. Lord Sinclair.
The Hon. Claude George Hay, M.P.
Sir Andrew N. Agnew, Bart., M.P.
Sir Lewis MacIver, Bart., M.P.
Sir George MacPherson Grant, Bart., of Ballindalloch.

Sir Alexander Keith Fraser, Bart.
Sir A. C. MacKenzie, Mus. Doc.
General Sir Ian Hamilton, K.C.B., D.S.O.
The Ven. Wm. MacDonald Sinclair, Archdeacon of Lond.
A. Bignold, Esq., M.P.
Colonel J. M. Denny, M.P.
Michael Hugh Shaw Stewart, Esq., M.P.
A. Ritchie, Esq., J.P., C.C.
G. N. Forbes, Esq.
W. D. MacKenzie, Esq., of Farr.

SCOTTISH CLANS' STRING & PIPE BAND.
Particulars of Practice, etc., may be obtained from the Hon. Secretaries.

SCOTTISH CLANS' LITERARY SOCIETY.
Meetings on alternate Wednesdays of every month from October to March, inclusive.

SCOTTISH CLANS' SHINTY CLUB.
Particulars of practice, etc., may be obtained from the Hon. Secretaries.

2nd August 1902.

Dear Mr Grant,

I really don't know what you will be thinking about me not answering your kind letters long ere this; I have been up to my eyes in work ever since you left. Russell and myself have many a laugh over your visit; I think that old nag going to the Station on Sunday night put the finishing tip to things.

No doubt you will be thinking it very strange not receiving your cheque yet. I only received it yesterday and have sent it to the Secretary to be signed I will have it back tomorrow and will send it on to you. It is made out for £5 ,, 10 . your letter

Letter to Grant from William Fraser, 2 Aug 1902, page 1.

89

keep the lot and I will square things up when I go north. I expect to be in Inverness about the 20th of this month.

I had a letter from my mother; herself and my father were delighted with your visit

Neil and his wife wishes to be kindly remembered to you. Thanks very much for the papers you sent me. I understand A. C. Mackenzie and his gamey wife are in Inverness just now. He will likely give you a call

This is a holiday in London but as I had so many things to do one way and another I did not go away. The weather here is very cold and wet — not a bit like the beginning of August.

I am enclosing you a copy of the London Scotsman with an account of the Concert.

Here goes the Principle Russell and I him may a chat over it.

I will send you a few line enclosed with the Cheque tomorrow

With kind regard.

Believe me.

Yours Sincerely

William Mackenzie Fraser

Letter to Grant from William Fraser, 2 Aug 1902, page 2.

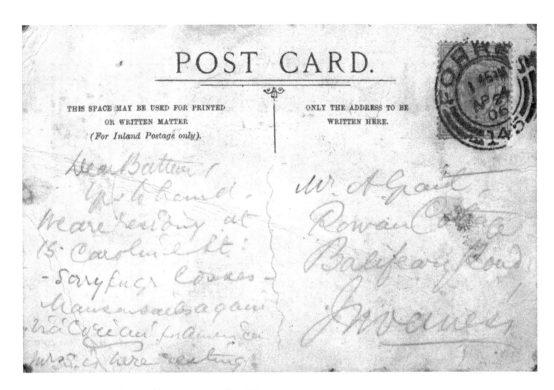

Postcard to Grant from Skinner, 24 April 1906.

Private

𝕭𝖗𝖔𝖔𝖒𝖜𝖊𝖑𝖑 𝕮𝖔𝖙𝖙𝖆𝖌𝖊,
𝕸𝖔𝖓𝖎𝖐𝖎𝖊,
𝖇𝖞 𝕯𝖚𝖓𝖉𝖊𝖊.

October 4th
1906

Dear Mr Grant -
        I had a letter
from Mr McIntosh
asking if Mr Skinner
was free for Nov 16th
the date of your Competition.
Well, he is free for that date
& if you can give him
£ 8-8- for Judging, &
playing two solos, then,

Letter to Grant from Skinner's wife.

92

he can come, but not for less money. Every Committee seems to think he should practically give his services. These people do not consider his age, & that he has his living to make. I am speaking to you as a friend, which I have proved you to be! My husband has been to Orkney & Shetland for

a fortnight with an Aberdeen Coy & is now in London making more records on the phonograph. He was sent for specially, the Coy defraying all expenses & paying him £10 - a day for three days.

I have been laid to one side again, but feel better today. Mamson has been at home since June doing nothing & I have never in the ten years ~~seen~~ I have known them seen a copper coin of

Letter to Grant from Skinner's wife, 4 Oct 1906, pages 2 & 3.

his money! All this has
told on my health until
it is utterly broken down.
I trust you are all well
& with warmest regards

Believe me
Yours Sincerely
G. May Kirk-Skinner

Letter to Grant from Skinner's wife, 4 Oct 1906, page 4.

THE ABBEY,
FORT-AUGUSTUS.
SCOTLAND.

Feb 12th 1928

Dear Mr Grant

I hope you got
back to Inverness yesterday morning, if
not Friday night, quite safely & with
the minimum of discomfort.

Will you please, on the first oppor-
-tunity that presents itself, convey to
all your musical accomplices my most
heartfelt thanks & the thanks of all of us
present at the Concert for your very
delightful & inspiriting – & I may say
"inspiring – music & presence at that
Concert which made it so great a success:
It will be a long time before we shall
leave off talking about that music.
We expected much & received more!
To yourself especially I would give
my warmest thanks. It was most

Letter to Grant from Ronald Alexander, 12 Feb 1928, page 1.

95

speaking of you to come on you did on
such a night & after such a distress-
-ing misadventure. I still have
the impression that you flew over
Loch Tulla with your violin tucked
under a wing!

The Rev A. L. Carg. Elwes greatly
hopes to meet you & your Strathspey
Band at the Town Hall next Friday
on the occasion of the Scouts' Concert.
I greatly, too, want you to hear
our Boys' Orchestra of which we are
rather proud. A very few years ago it
had no existence. But I wish you
could teach them to add Strathspeys
to their other beautiful items!

Strathspeys, to my mind, besides their
beautiful music, are the Folk Music
of a great race & charged with the
spirit of the Highland Race. Like
the Gaelic Songs they are incomparable.
With my fond wish to you & John Fraser
& all of the Society, Believe me
Yours ever heartily, Ronald Alexander.

Letter to Grant from Ronald Alexander, 12 Feb 1928, page 2.

Bonnington
Tarland
Aberdeenshire
5ᵗʰ April 1931

Dear Batten

At the first meeting of the Scott Skinner
Memorial Committee, I proposed that Peter Milne
should be included, and part of the money raised to be
given for a memorial to Peter, but my proposal was
turned down. I suppose the reason was that there was
only one other man and myself present who knew
Peter Milne personally.

I came to Tarland three weeks ago
and am teaching here, and as Tarland is Peter Milne's
native place, the idea occurred to me that it would be
very appropriate to have a committee formed in
this district, and I am pleased to say I have been
successful in getting a Committee formed to raise
a Fund for a memorial to Peter Milne. It is 23
years since Peter died, and there is nothing on his grave.
The Committee are: - Chairman Wᵐ J. B. Anderson

Letter to Grant from George Rose Wood, 5 April 1931, page 1.

97

Schoolhouse, Logie Coldstone, and Messrs
G Rose Wood, Aberdeen; A.R. Henderson, Torphins;
John Knowles, Ballater; Wm Anderson, Tarland;
and Alex Innes, Tarland.

       I am enclosing a Subscription
Sheet, and we shall be very grateful of your assistance.
I am sure a good many members of your Band would
give a small subscription. Could you not get up a
Concert in Aid of this Fund in some small Town in
your district, such as Muir of Ord, or Beauly. I Am
organising a Series of Concerts in this district in aid
of the Fund. The Opening Concert is fixed for the 24th April
at Tarland. The Aberdeen Strathspey & Reel Society
Band are coming to the Tarland Concert. I am also
arranging for Concerts at Logie Coldstone, Dinnet,
Towie and Strathdon.

       Our object in raising this Fund is to
get a modest Memorial Stone for Peter Milne's grave and
to publish all his unpublished Music. The best of
Peter's Compositions are unpublished. I have a
number of them, but since I came to Tarland Mr

Letter to Grant from George Rose Wood, 5 April 1931, page 2.

Also Innes Boot Maker, who was a pupil of Peter and a great friend and enthusiast, has shown me a whole lot of Peter's unpublished compositions that I had never seen before, some of them very pretty; particularly "Bonnie Aboyne". I will send you a copy of this beautiful melody. I am to play it at the Concerts. It would be a great pity to allow these beautiful unpublished melodies of Peter's to get lost, as no doubt they would if they are not published.

I have written a short history of Peter Milne's life, which will appear in the Aberdeen Press and Journal, I expect tomorrow, so look out for it. Peter Milne was extremely modest, kind hearted, and a most lovable man. I have sent a photo of Peter's to the Press which will appear if they manage to reproduce it.

I hope you are keeping well, And with kindest regards

Yours faithfully
G Rose Wood

Letter to Grant from George Rose Wood, 5 April 1931, page 3.

5 Telford Terrace

4 Aug. 904

Dear Mr Grant.

Mr T. Miller has just sent me word that he had overlooked an important engagement when he promised to call on me on Friday, so that we perhaps had better put off the meeting in the meantime.

I hope the pain in your eyes has completely gone.

With kind regards.

Yours sincerely

And. MacIntosh

Letter to Grant from Andrew MacIntosh, 4 Aug 1904.

The Cottage,

Elsing, Dereham.

5th March. 1925.

62 Oxford St

London W.

My. Dear Baton.

What. do you think
of. your. vibration system now.

It is only the story from Croft.
to University!

How are you getting on I
have not heard anything of you for
so long that I am beginning to wonder
what. your old face is like, Do you
have as many visitors as ever, I
read in the Inverness Courier
some time ago that you are still going
strong, I may be in the north for a
few days shortly, so string up your
old. fiddle, in Holland Park form

Letter to Grant from W. M. Fraser, 5 March 1925, page 1.
This letter dated 5 March 1925 was sent to Grant by his friend William MacKenzie Fraser, one time
Honorary Treasurer of the London Inverness-shire Association. Mr. MacKenzie sends his regards
and asks whether there have been further developments with the 'Grant Vibration Rod'. He also
enquires after 'The Strathspey King', Scott Skinner.

not forgetting old Neil Mackay and the Pipers
from the Caledonian School that went to
sleep in the bath instead of his bed, and the
old jobber who went up the hill backwards

Alick Mackenzie is up north somewhere
between Aviemore & Inverness

Did you do anything further about
your vibration Bow, you ought to

I called over to see the Ritchies some
time ago, both the boys are married
and the poor old mother died some
time ago,

Any word of the King I have
not heard about him for some
time

With kindest regards to
all at home from your
Auld friend
William Mackenzie Fraser,

Letter to Grant from W. M. Fraser, 5 March 1925, page 2.

London Inverness-shire Association.

President · The MACKINTOSH OF MACKINTOSH.

Vice-Presidents:

THE RIGHT HON. LORD LOVAT.
SIR ROBERT B. FINLAY, K.C., M.P.
SIR GEORGE MACPHERSON GRANT, BART.
SIR JOHN STIRLING-MAXWELL, BART., M.P.
DONALD CAMERON, Esq., of Lochiel,
    Lord Lieutenant of Inverness-shire.
SIR DONALD CURRIE, G.C.M.G.
JAMES E. B. BAILLIE, Esq., of Dochfour.

W. D. MACKENZIE, Esq., of Farr and Newbie.
THE BISHOP OF ARGYLL AND THE ISLES.
THE VEN. W. MACDONALD SINCLAIR, D.D.,
    Archdeacon of London.
A. LEE INNES, Esq.
THE REV. DR. DONALD MACLEOD, M.A.
MACLEOD of Macleod.
THE RT. HON. LORD TWEEDMOUTH.

THE REV. ALBERT V. BAILLIE, M.A.
CHARLES CLARK, Esq.
ANGUS MACKINTOSH, Esq., of Holme.
The Right Honourable LORD STRATHCONA and
    MOUNT ROYAL, G.C.M.G.; P.C.
W. SOPPER, Esq., of Dunmaglass.
RUARI C. GOODEN-CHISHOLM, Esq.
COLONEL JOHN S. YOUNG.

Honorary Treasurers:
DONALD C. FRASER, 24, KING STREET, HAMMERSMITH, W.
W. MACKENZIE FRASER, 9, CLARENDON ROAD, HOLLAND PARK, W.

Honorary Secretaries:
JAMES DOAK, 16, MARK LANE, E.C.
DONALD H. FRASER, 6, RANGOON STREET, E.C.

14th April 1902

Dear Mr. Grant,

The London Inverness-shire Ass'n
are going to hold a Concert in the Queens Hall
on the 3rd July.

I have suggested to the Committee that
you should be asked to give a selection
of Highland music on the Violon

I have heard you play several times
and feel sure that you would take well.

Will you kindly let me know & return
if you would be willing to come and
what your expenses would be.

Have you heard that your friend

Letter to Grant from W. M. Fraser, 14 April 1902, page 1.

This letter dated 14 April 1902 was sent to Grant from William MacKenzie Fraser, at that time Honorary Treasurer of the London Inverness-shire Association. In the letter, Mr. Fraser invites Mr. Grant to perform at a forthcoming concert in the Queens Hall, London.

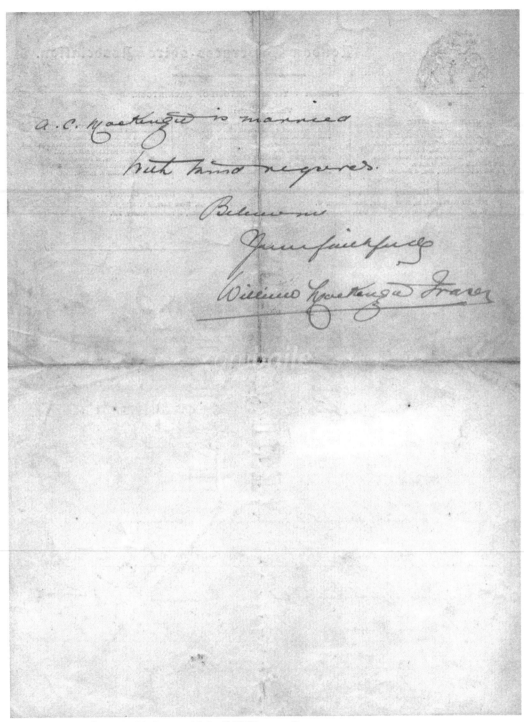

A. C. Mackenzie is married

with kind regards.

Believe me

Yours faithfully

William Mackenzie Fraser

Letter to Grant from W. M. Fraser, 14 April 1902, page 2 .

25th Sept. 1935

Subscription list in aid of a
wreath etc in memory of the late
Mr. David McCaskill by members
of the Highland Strathspey & Reel Society

Alex. Grant	Paid	5	.
I. McPherson	Paid	5	.
Duncan Grant	Paid	5	.
Hugh McDonald	Paid	5	.
E. C. Jack	Paid	5	.
Donald Riddell	Paid	4	.
B. G. Hoare	Paid	2	6
Ian Grant	Paid	3	.
Wm Fraser, Muirtown	Paid	2	6
Rod. Mackenzie	Paid	2	6
K. Tuach	Paid	2	6
Peter McDonald, Loch Duich Hotel	Paid	2	6
Secretary	Paid		
Wm Mackay, Clachnaharry	Paid	2	6
Wm Davidson	Paid	2	6
George Bell	Paid	2	6
Duncan Cameron "County"	Paid	5	.
John Brown	Paid	2	6
Tom. Gordon	Paid	2	6
James Morrison Gair	Paid	2	6
James Ritchie	Paid	2	6
James McBean	Paid	2	6
Wm Mackay	Paid	2	6
J. D. Wheatley	Paid	2	6
Alex. Fraser & John Fraser	Paid	5	.
D. Morison, Beauly	Paid	10	-
F. McDougall	Paid	2	6
Per Duncan Grant 1 Friend	Paid	5	.
Duncan Mackenzie, do. Creetown	Paid	2	6
Arthur Mackenzie	Paid	2	6
Chas. Lemon	Paid	2	6
	£	5 12	.

Highland Strathspey & Reel Society, accounts sheet, 1935.

105

Strathspey and Reel Societies have been a common feature of the traditional music scene in Scotland since the formation of the first society in Edinburgh in 1881. The Highland branch was formed in 1903. One of its founder members, Alexander Grant (also known as 'Battan') was leader of the society right up until his death in 1942, a period of almost forty years.

This accounts sheet dated 25 September 1935 shows a subscription list in aid of a wreath etc., in memory of the late Mr. David McCaskill. Donations from members of the Highland Strathspey and Reel Society amount to £5 12s. Included in the list are donations from Alexander Grant and Donald Riddell, and Donald Morison.

Croy Concert
6th April 1978

PROGRAMME.
+0-0-0-0-0-0-0-0-

PART 1.

1.	Highland Selections	....	Highland Strathspey & Reel Society.
2.	Song	....	Mr. James MacKenzie.
3.	Song	....	Miss MacLeod.
4.	Song	....	~~Mr. A. MacDonald~~ MR. C. MILLER
5.	Song	....	Mrs. C. MacLeod.
6.	Violin Selections	....	Mr. Alex. Grant.
7.	*Harmony Quartette* Song	....	Miss Munro
8.	Song	....	Mr. Black.

PART. 11.

1.	Highland Selections	....	Highland Strathspey & Reel Society.
2.	Song	....	~~Mr. A. Gibb~~ *J. MacLeod*
3.	Song	....	Mrs. C. MacLeod.
4.	Song	....	Mr. J. MacKenzie.
5.	Song	....	Miss MacLeod.
6.	Violin Selections.	....	Mr. Alex. Grant. *Quartett*
7.	*Sel.* Song	....	Miss Munro.
8.	Song	....	Mr. Black.
9.	Highland Selections	....	Highland Strathspey & Reel Society.

Highland Strathspey & Reel Society, Competition Programme 1905, page 3.

This typed programme is for a Highland Strathspey and Reel Concert at Croy, 6th April 1928. The programme includes solo violin performances from Alexander Grant and songs from various people including Miss MacLeod and Mr. Black. The society opens and closes the concert with 'Highland Selections'

Highland Strathspey & Reel Society Programme, 1932, page 1.

This programme is for a Highland Strathspey and Reel Society Concert held on 21 June 1932, in the Central Hall, Academy Street, Inverness. The society's chairman at this time was ex-Baillie George Gallon.

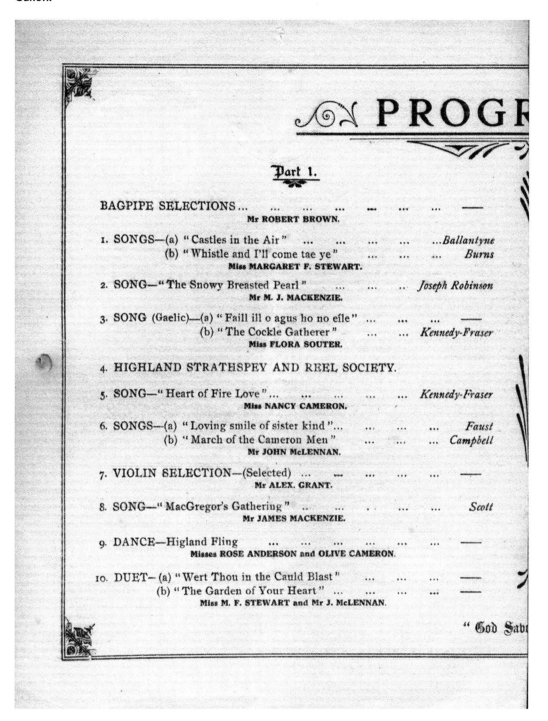

Highland Strathspey & Reel Society Programme, 1932, page 2.

This programme is for a Highland Strathspey and Reel Society Concert held on 21 June 1932, in the Central Hall, Academy Street, Inverness. As well as leading the fiddlers (item 4), Mr. Grant performed a solo violin selection (item 7).

RAMME

Part 2.

BAGPIPE SELECTIONS ...   .   —
Mr ROBERT BROWN.

1. PIANO SELECTION ...   .   —
Miss FLORA SOUTER.

2. VIOLIN SELECTIONS   ...   .   ——
Mr ALEX. GRANT.

3. SONG —"There's a Land"   ...   .   —
Mr JAMES MACKENZIE.

4. DANCE—Sword ...   .   —
Misses ANDERSON and CAMERON.

5. HIGHLAND STRATHSPEY AND REEL SOCIETY.

6. SONG—"I'm Owre Young tae Marry Yet" ...   .   *Burns*
Miss NANCY CAMERON.

7. SONG—"My Nannie's Awa" ...   .   *Burns*
Mr M. J. MACKENZIE

8. SONG— "Flora Macdonald's Lament"   ...   .   —
Miss M. F. STEWART.

9. SONG—(a) "Sound the Pibroch"   ...   .   *Macleod*
   (b) "Standard on the Braes o' Mar"   ...   .   *Laing*
Mr J. McLENNAN.

the King."

Highland Strathspey & Reel Society Programme, 1932, page 3.
This programme is for a Highland Strathspey and Reel Society Concert held on 21 June 1932, in the Central Hall, Academy Street, Inverness. As well as leading the fiddlers (item 5), Mr. Grant performed a solo violin selection (item 2).

Highland Strathspey & Reel Society Programme, 1932, page 4 (advert).

This advert for 'Mrs David Logan, Pianoforte and Music Seller' appeared on the back of a programme for a Highland Strathspey and Reel Society Concert held on 21 June 1932, in the Central Hall, Academy Street, Inverness.

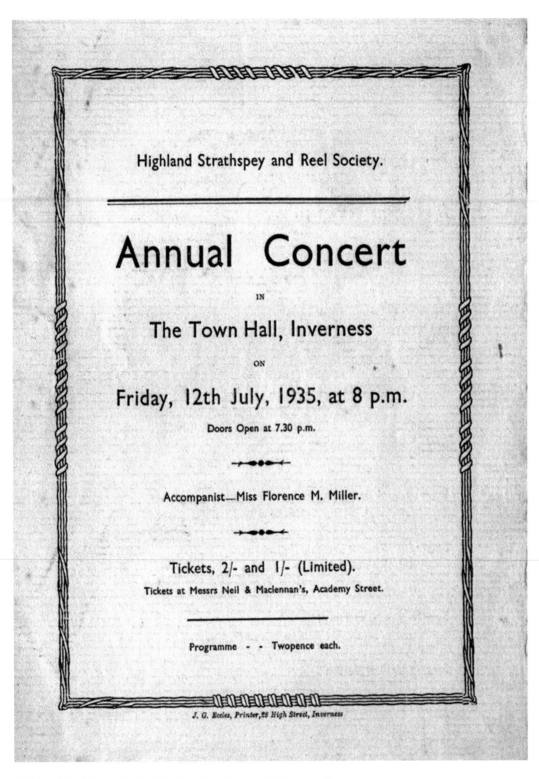

Highland Strathspey and Reel Society.

Annual Concert

IN

The Town Hall, Inverness

ON

Friday, 12th July, 1935, at 8 p.m.

Doors Open at 7.30 p.m.

Accompanist—Miss Florence M. Miller.

Tickets, 2/- and 1/- (Limited).

Tickets at Messrs Neil & Maclennan's, Academy Street.

Programme - - Twopence each.

J. G. Eccles, Printer, 28 High Street, Inverness

Highland Strathspey & Reel Society Programme, 1935, page 1.

This programme is for a Highland Strathspey and Reel Society Concert held on 12 July 1935 in the Town Hall, Inverness. Tickets are priced at one and two shillings and the accompanist is Miss Florence M. Miller.

PROGF

PART I.

1. **Bagpipe Selections** ... ... ———
Pipe-Major John Macdonald, M.B.E.

2. **Song** (Gaelic)—" Fear a Bhata " ... ... *Traditional*
Miss Mary Macdonald.

3. **Song**—" Border Ballad " ... ... *Cowan*
Mr Fred Miller.

4. **March**—" Balmoral Highlanders " ... ... ———
Strathspeys—" Highlanders Farewell " ... ... ———
" Miss Drummond of Perth " ... ... ———
" George the Fourth " ... ... ———
Reels—" George the Fourth " ... ... ———
" Cabar Feidh " ... ... ———
Highland Strathspey and Reel Society.

5. **Song**—" Bonnie Strathyre " ... ... *Songs of the North*
Mrs J. Thow.

6. **Dance**—Sword Dance ... ... ———
Miss Olive Cameron.

7. **Songs**—(a) " Silent Worship " ... ... *Handel*
(b) " There is a Ladye " ... ... *Winifred Bury*
Mr M. J. Mackenzie.

8. **Song**—" The Misty Isle of Skye " ... ... *Grimshaw*
Miss Peggy Strachan.

9. **Song**—" Maid of Morven " ... ... *Songs of the North*
Mr Wm. Fraser.

Highland Strathspey & Reel Society Programme, 1932, page 2.

This programme is for a Highland Strathspey and Reel Society Concert held on 12 July 1935 in the Town Hall, Inverness. It includes various solo artists including Pipe Major John Macdonald M.B.E.

113

PART II.

1. **Bagpipe Selections** ... ... —
   Pipe-Major John Macdonald, M.B.E.

2. **Song**—"Lassie o' Mine" ... ... *Mackenzie Murdoch*
   Mrs J. Thow.

3. **Song**—"My Land" ... ... *W. S. Roddie*
   Mr Fred Miller.

4. **Song** (Gaelic)—"Far an robh mi 'n Raoir" ... ... *Neil McLeod*
   Miss Mary Macdonald.

5. **March**—"Scott Skinner's Welcome to Inverness" ... ... —
   Strathspeys—"Miss Lyall" ... ... —
       "Highland Whisky" ... ... —
       "Lady Madeline Sinclair" ... ... —
   Reels—"The Mason's Apron" ... ... —
       "Perth Hunt" ... ... —
   Highland Strathspey and Reel Society.

6. **Song**—"Land of Hope and Glory" ... ... *Elgar*
   Mr Wm. Fraser.

7. **Song**—"Just a Cottage small" ... ... —
   Miss Peggy Strachan.

8. **Dance**—Highland Fling ... ... —
   Miss Olive Cameron.

9. **Songs**—(a) "The Auld Fisher" ... ... *Hamish McCunn*
       (b) "Joy of my Heart" ... ... *Hugh S. Roberton*
   Mr M. J. Mackenzie.

GOD SAVE THE KING.

Highland Strathspey & Reel Society Programme, 1935, page 3.

This programme is for a Highland Strathspey and Reel Society Concert held on 12 July 1935 in the Town Hall, Inverness. Included in the programme are solo vocal performances by Miss Mary Macdonald and Miss Peggy Strachan.

Highland Strathspey & Reel Society Programme, 1935, page 4.

This advert for the Glen Albyn and County Hotels appeared on the back of a programme for a Highland Strathspey and Reel Society Concert held on 12 July 1935 in the Town Hall, Inverness.

ROYAL BURGH OF INVERNESS

TELEGRAPHIC ADDRESS
"TOWN CLERK"
TELEPHONE N°43.

JAMES CAMERON,
TOWN CLERK.

Town Clerk's Office,
Town House,
Inverness 31st August, 1936.

DMR/MF.

Mr John Fraser,
 Secretary,
  Highland Strathspey & Reel Society,
   Telford Terrace,
    INVERNESS.

Dear Sir,

<u>Ness Islands.</u>

I have to inform you that the Entertainments Committee have arranged to hold two further Special Nights in the Ness Islands on 4th and 11th prox., and there is also a possibility that a Special Night will be held on 18th prox. in aid of the funds of the Royal Northern Infirmary. I shall therefore be glad if you can kindly arrange for the attendance of your Society to sustain the programmes on these dates.

Yours faithfully,

Town Clerk.

Letter to Secretary of Highland Strathspey & Reel Society, 1936.

In this letter dated 31 August 1936, from the Inverness Town Clerk, J. Cameron to the society's secretary, John Fraser, a request is being made for the society's attendance at three evening concerts arranged by the council's Entertainments Committee.

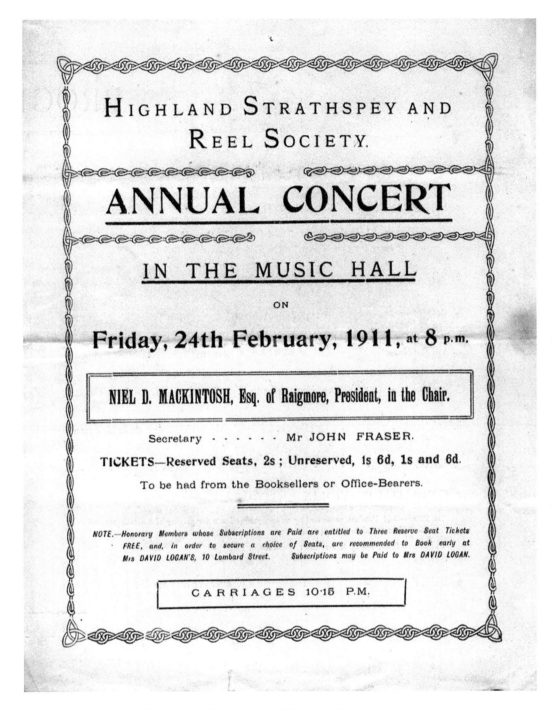

Highland Strathspey & Reel Society Programme, 1911, page 1.

This programme is for a Highland Strathspey and Reel Society Annual Concert held on 24 February 1911, in the Music Hall, Inverness. At this time, the society's president was Neil D. Mackintosh of Raigmore. Concert tickets are priced at two shillings, one and sixpence, and sixpence.

... PROGR

PART I.

1. SELECTION - - - - HIGHLAND STRATHSPEY AND REEL SOCIETY

   Strathspeys—"Lady Mary Ramsay," "Jessie Smith," "Cameron got his Wife Again."
   Reels—"Jenny Dang the Weaver," "The Wind that Shakes the Barley."

2. SONG - - - "My Nannie, O" - - Mr DOUGLAS YOUNG

3. SONG - - - "Eileen Alannah" Miss JESSIE LIVINGSTONE

4. VIOLIN SOLO - - - Mr ALEX. GRANT, Leader of H.S. and R.S.

5. SONG - "Tell me, Mary, how to Woo Thee" Mr DONALD FRASER

6. DANCE - - - "Highland Fling" Messrs MACPHERSON & MACNEILL

7. SONG - - - - - - Miss KATE MACDONALD

8. COMPETITION—VIOLIN

   1st Prize—Gold Pendant, presented by an anonymous donor for playing of a Strathspey and
   Reel of Scott Skinner's compositions.
   2nd Prize—Presented by Messrs Marr Wood & Co.

9. DUET - - - Miss JESSIE LIVINGSTONE and Mr DOUGLAS YOUNG

ACCOMPANIST - - - -

Highland Strathspey & Reel Society Programme, 1911, page 2.

This programme is for a Highland Strathspey and Reel Society Annual Concert held on 24 February 1911, in the Music Hall, Inverness. As well as leading the fiddlers (item 1), Mr. Grant performs a violin solo (item 4).

...AMME ...

PART II.

1. SONG - - - "Macgregor's Gathering" - Mr Douglas Young

2. SELECTION - - - - Highland Strathspey and Reel Society

    Strathspeys—" Miller of Drone," "South of the Grampians" " Earl Gray."
    Reels —" Mrs Macleod of Raasay," "High Road to Linton."

3. SONG - - - "Il Bacio " (*Arditi*) - Miss Jessie Livingstone

4 COMPETITION—PIANO - Strathspeys and Reels by any Composer
    1st Prize—Gold Medal—Presented by Highland Strathspey and Reel Society.
    2nd Prize—Collection of Music, value 15s—Presented by Messrs Logan & Co., Church Street.

5. SONG - "Doon the Burn, Davie, Lad " Miss Kate Macdonald

6. DANCE - - Highland Reel ⎰Misses M. Fraser and W. Macneill
                                    ⎱Messrs Macpherson and Macneill

7. SONG - - - "Good-Bye" (*Tosti*) Miss Jessie Livingstone

PRESENTATION OF PRIZES.

8. SONG - - - "The Distant Shore" - - Mr Douglas Young

9. VIOLIN SOLO - - - - Mr A. Grant, Leader of H.S. and R.S.

- - - Mrs WHITEHEAD.

Highland Strathspey & Reel Society Programme, 1911, page 3.

This programme is for a Highland Strathspey and Reel Society Annual Concert held on 24 February 1911, in the Music Hall, Inverness. As well as leading the fiddlers (item 2), Mr. Grant concludes the evening with a violin solo (item 9).

Academy Street showing the Empire Theatre or Picture House

(Courtesy of Inverness Field Club – Old Inverness in Pictures)

To the Members of the
Highland Strathspey & Reel Society.

1

I have gone carefully over the Document embodying the donor's money gift to establish a "competition" in Strathspeys and Reels by the Highland Strathspey & Reel Society and have to make the following remarks thereanent:

The object the donor has mainly in view appears to be to aim at perfect playing, to recover old tunes and encourage the production of new. — Three entirely different departments, demanding separate gifts and abilities. As such it is collectively outwith the scope and possibilities of a Society of players, whose business and purport is to produce musical rendering.

The Society therefore must per se decline a competition in which original composition or literary research are made conditions. These involve special gifts and advantages in which individual members of a collective body can hardly

Letter to Members of Highland Strathspey & Reel Society, 1927, page 1.

This letter (page 1) to the Highland branch from Mr. B.G. Hoare, dated 21 October 1927, refers to a sum of money donated to the society for the establishment of a competition in 'Strathspeys and Reels'. It is Mr. Hoare's opinion that the society decline the offer; the donor adds too many restrictive conditions. Mr. Hoare concludes by conjecturing whether the donor is, in fact, a local celebrity.

be expected to be (endowed). Originality ²
in any form belongs only to genius
and is extremely rare.

With regard to the playing rules,
I would again remark that you cannot
go outside the rules that apply to an
Art itself. Tradition and practice has
already fixed the forms of both Strathspey
and Reel. You may take a different
type of setting, say Neil Gow's, Kerr's
or Scott-Skinner's (the latter the best
undoubtedly for reasons, which I can't
enter into at present) but you cannot "Vary"
it without destroying its content as a
dance tune. Variations are reserved for
Marches, (Pibrochs) Laments (Coronachs)
+c. Here you have a slow air which
can be "varied" in notation and "time"
without destroying its form. The Strathspey
and Reel demand absolute conformity
to its pattern throughout, fixed by the laws
of its own content and purpose.

Changes of key as tests of musicianship

Letter to Members of Highland Strathspey & Reel Society, 1927, page 2.

are quite practicable. Only, it should be born in mind that the reason that two sharps (D major) and three sharps (A major) are most commonly used is the facility that both these keys afford to the player where rapid bowing and full toned notes are desirable.

It would be an easy matter to make a number of sets a full test of playing ability, but here again there must be a minimum — selection of new or old or difficult sets is another matter — as time and numbers are factors even in competition.

I think the donor's own remark; "Our endeavour is that the collection and the Competition, will be so difficult that the Medal will seldom or ever be won" is a correct summing up of the whole matter viz Impossibility.

Should this however happen the testator has a way out of the difficulty:
" No member can have more than one Gold Medal,
" And in the event of the Gold Medallist winning

Letter to Members of Highland Strathspey & Reel Society, 1927, page 3.

"again, he gets a gold Bar each time he   4
" wins and to be attached to the gold medal".

How this can be done with £10, is an enigma to me. The interest on £10 after buying the first medal would be ——— a few pence.

Viewing the whole scheme, I think it is the duty of the Highland Strathspey & Reel Society to decline its acceptance, as it cannot carry out its provisions. Unless the donor comes forward and agrees to let the Society draw up its own ideas in rules to govern such a competition.

The name Jomson (or Johnson?) and the anonymity attached to the "document" makes one wonder if the Society is being "hagged" under the pseudonym of a local celebrity.

B[?] Hoare

Inverness 21 Oct 1927.

Letter to Members of Highland Strathspey & Reel Society, 1927, page 4.

Copy of letter.

"Netherdale,
Beauly
22nd Mar./28.

Dear Monsieur,

Many thanks for the copy of the Ayrshire Post with report of meeting of the Ayr Sketch Club.

I am very much astonished at the way Mr. Nash is reported to have represented his connection with Mr. Grant's Rondello for we who have been watching the development of the instrument during the past number of years know quite well that it was not merely the idea which originated with Mr. Grant, but that every detail of material, size and structure was worked out with the utmost exactness by him.

We understand that all these had been

Letter on Alexander Grant's 'Rondello', 22 March 1928, page 1.

This copy letter dated 22 March 1928, from Thomas Macdonald to D. Morison, Assistant Leader of the Highland Strathspey and Reel Society, refers to the 'Rondello', a disc-shaped violin invented by Alexander Grant, Inverness. It appears that in a recent copy of the 'Ayrshire Post', a fiddle-maker by the name of Nash has been laying claim to the invention of the 'Rondello'. Mr. Macdonald suggests the article be brought to the attention of the Highland Strathspey and Reel Society.

been sent to Nash and that he merely made a copy to measurements and instructions, as any mechanic might do.

Now, anyone who did not know the circumstances, reading the report in the Ayr paper would come to the conclusion that Nash was the man who invented the instrument (it says "made and named by him") on a hint from Grant, which you and I know to be sheer bunkum.

Why do you not bring the report before the Strathspey & Reel Society the members of which, of course, know about Mr. Grant's invention? Surely they will rise to the occasion and do something to make it clear to the world that any credit is due to their veteran leader and to the town of Inverness and not of Ayr.

Yours etc.

(Signed) Thos. Macdonald."

Letter on Alexander Grant's 'Rondello', 22 March 1928, page 2.

This copy letter dated 22 March 1928, from Thomas Macdonald to D. Morison, Assistant Leader of the Highland Strathspey and Reel Society, refers to the 'Rondello', a disc-shaped violin invented by Alexander Grant, Inverness. It appears that in a recent copy of the 'Ayrshire Post', a fiddle-maker by the name of Nash has been laying claim to the invention of the 'Rondello'. Mr. Macdonald suggests the article be brought to the attention of the Highland Strathspey and Reel Society.

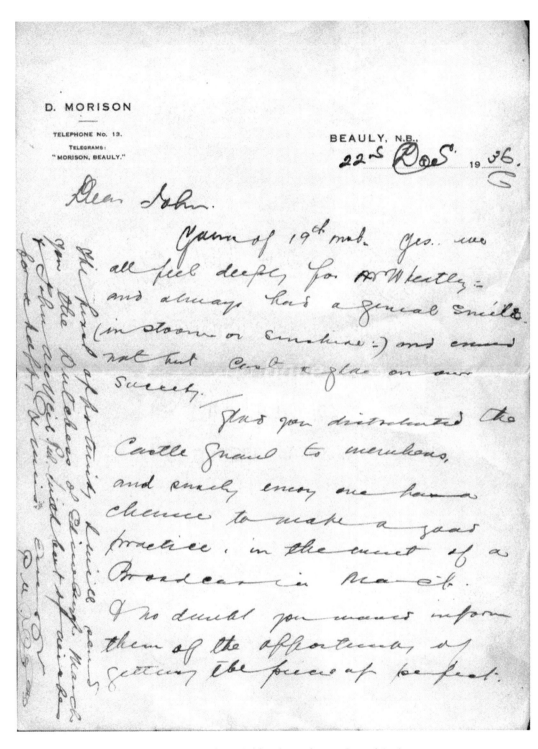

D. MORISON

TELEPHONE No. 13.
TELEGRAMS:
"MORISON, BEAULY."

BEAULY, N.B.,
22ᵈ Dec. 19 36.

Dear John,

Yours of 19ᵗʰ inst. Yes.. we all feel deeply for Mr Wheatley:– and always had a genial smile (in storm or sunshine :–) and could not but cast a glow on our society.

Glad you distributed the Castle Grant to members, and surely every one has a chance to make a good practice, in the event of a Broadcast in March. I no doubt you would inform them of the opportunity of getting the piece up perfect.

Letter from D. Morison, Assistant Leader, Highland Strathspey & Reel Society.

This letter dated 22 December 1936 is from the Highland branch Assistant Leader, Mr. D. Morison of Beauly, to 'John' (probably John Fraser, Secretary). Mr. Morison mentions three pieces of music; 'Castle Grant', 'The Duchess of Edinburgh' (march), and the 'John McNeill Reel'.

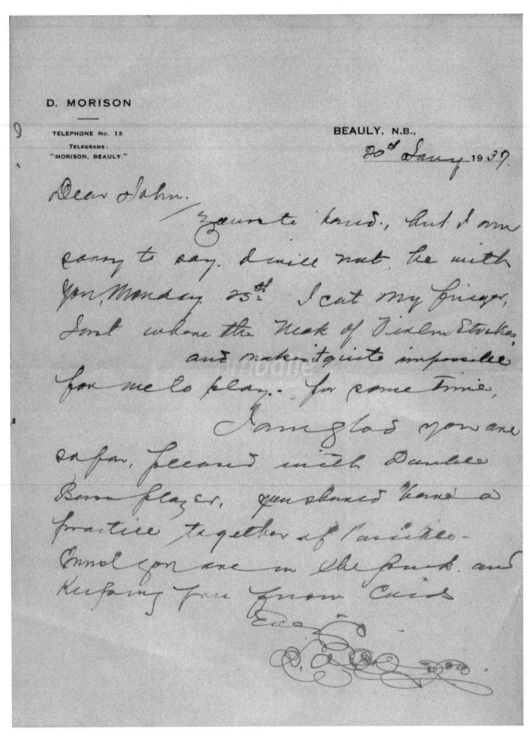

Letter from D. Morison, Assistant Leader, Highland Strathspey & Reel Society.

This letter dated 20 January 1937 is from the Highland branch Assistant Leader, Mr. D. Morison of Beauly, to 'John' (probably John Fraser, Secretary). In it, Mr. Morison explains he cannot attend the next concert as he has cut his finger and is unable to play.

Letter from D. Morison, Assistant Leader, Highland Strathspey & Reel Society.

This letter dated 28 November 1936 is from the Highland branch Assistant Leader, Mr. D. Morison of Beauly, to 'John' (probably John Fraser, Secretary). In it, Mr. Morison explains he has received, from Alexander Grant, a simpler way of playing 'Spey in a Spate', one of Scott Skinner's compositions.

Crosbie H°
Monkton
Prestwick   14/3/'37

To the Sec
    Inverness H.S.&R.S.

        Many thanks for the copies of y. M. Henderson's
7/8 So. Melodies, I have had a job getting them.
Bayley & Ferguson to me they were out of print,
so I thought of Mr Grant and as the Yankees
say, "everything is all right." I enclose P.G.
for Books & Postage. Thanking you very
much again for the trouble you have taken
to send them to me. The Ayr S. & R. Soc
told their 2nd Annual Concert in the
town Hall on Wednesday 17th. I trust
you have had a good season, I have only
been out playing once this season, that was
at the Kilmarnock S. & R. Soc on the 24th Feb.
My Boss is a Semi Cripple now and requires two
to help him every time he moves, Kind regards
to Mr Grant and fraternal Greetings to Inverness H. S. & R. Soc. not forgetting yourself.

                I am
                Your's Sincerely

                Jas. T. McEwen.

Letter to Secretary, Highland Strathspey & Reel Society, 14 March 1937.

This letter dated 14 March 1937 is from James P. McEwen of Prestwick to the Secretary of the Highland Strathspey & Reel Society in Inverness. Mr. McEwen, a member of the Ayr Strathspey and Reel Society, was recently sent a copy of 'Flowers of Scottish Melody' (1935) from the Highland branch. He encloses £6 to cover the cost of the book and postage, and sends his kind regards to the Highland branch and its Leader, Alexander Grant.

12 Polmuir Road,
Aberdeen
12/11/36.

Dear Mr Fraser,

Many thanks for your 30/- in P.O.'s. I'm to send order for 36 copies of the Skinner group to be posted straight to you.

Your later communication is funny. Mr Monson is not the first Scots fiddler to read some of my _alternative_ notes as chord notes. No chords are intended at all. Since your copy is slightly different from the one I sent you last, here is the most up-to-date set, with Mac's Strathspey in close attendance. Mind you, I think these two tunes should also be played together. It would save you & Mac. shaking hands so often (?). Pattais one would look fine after a pipe march. I'm really proud of all three tunes, so it's up to you all to add to my pride!

Reiterated thanks.

Please send them on to D. Monson

Yours sincerely,
Jn. Henderson

Letter to Secretary, Highland Strathspey & Reel Society, 12 Nov 1936.

This letter dated 12 November 1936 is from Jim Murdoch Henderson, Aberdeen, to the Highland branch Secretary, Mr. John Fraser. Mr. Henderson, himself a celebrated fiddler, composer and arranger, is acknowledging receipt of Mr. Fraser's order for sheet music - 36 copies of the recently published Scott Skinner group of tunes.

𝕳

12 Polmuir Road.
~~37 Westburn Road,~~
Aberdeen.
9 · 11 · 36.

Dear Mrs Fraser,

I had a letter from Battan some days ago saying that your society would take 3 doz. copies of my new Scott Skinner group at 10d. each – 30/- altogether. Please send me "official" tidings so that I can order the pieces right away. Bayley & Ferguson will think that I'm trying to do them in.

I've had the enclosed airs ready for over a week. I'm confident I've given Battan, Mac. & you three everlasting airs. You *must* get them all up for *me* also. You will have the honour to give Battan his one: he gave you yours. By the by, the set of your air found here – perhaps slightly different from what you already have – is the one that is to go down to posterity. In fact I shall probably sometimes change its key to Bb to suit some

Letter, Highland Strathspey & Reel Society, 9 Nov 1936, page 1.

135

This letter (page 1) dated 9 November 1936 is from Jim Murdoch Henderson, Aberdeen, to the Highland branch Secretary, Mr. John Fraser. Mr. Henderson, himself a celebrated fiddler, composer and arranger, is requesting an official order for sheet music recently (unofficially) requested by 'Battan'. He also encloses three recently composed 'everlasting airs' specifically for Mr. MacPherson, Mr. Fraser, and 'Battan' Grant.

groups. P.J. Hardie will broadcast it next year, I hope. Battan's tune is credited to be the best pipe strathspey composed since "Maggie Cameron". MacPherson's strathspey should sound very well indeed with the band. I have the habit of composing airs that are suitable more for good soloists rather than bands. The same cannot be said of any of the three airs now presented to the Big Three. Mac's air is a gem too.

I hope this note reaches you before your practice tomorrow so that you can break the news gently and compel all the players to take off their hats to you. Posterity will not have far to seek for a reason for my intimate association with your organisation. I always favour those who play for the sake of helping the cause rather than with the prime object of lining their own pockets. If I'm anything at all in music I'm patriotic and take much pleasure in considering you lot of enthusiasts the same.

Kindest regards to all.

Yours ever faithfully,
Murdoch Henderson

Letter, Highland Strathspey & Reel Society, 9 Nov 1936, page 2.

THE GLASGOW EVENING NEWS.

8 Dec. 1936.

Miss Alexander gave interpretations of these
songs which made the recital one of the most
interesting and enjoyable we have heard for
a long time.

The singerstone was always beautiful and her
outlook musical in every detail, in a long and
varied list of songs.   She gave us splendid
phrasing and real insight into the many moods
of the songs.

THE GLASGOW HERALD.

8 Dec. 1936.

Miss Alexander had previously won her place
in Glasgow as a pianist and it was equally
unlooked for and delightful to find her
displaying all the virtues of a fine singer
of Lieder.

In the thirty songs a considerable range of
mood was covered and always the result was
eloquent and made impressive by its sincerity.

This letter (page 1) dated 15 December 1936 is from Joan Alexander, L.R.A.M., A.R.C.M., to the Highland branch Secretary, Mr. John Fraser. Miss Alexander is an experienced soprano singer. She asks to be considered for an engagement with the society and encloses critiques from a recent recital in Glasgow.

CRAIGMONIE,

INVERNESS, 10th December, 1913.

Dear Sir,

     I am obliged for your letter of yesterday, informing me that the Highland Reel and Strathspey Society are to hold their annual concert on Thursday evening, 25th December (Christmas Day) in the Music Hall, and asking me to act as Chairman on the occasion. I am very sorry that I am unable to do so. For many years Mrs. Mackay and myself have had a gathering of relatives and friends on Christmas Day, and the invitations for the coming Christmas dinner have already been sent out.

          I am,

             Yours faithfully,

Mr. J. Fraser,
   3 Telford Terrace,
      INVERNESS.

Letter to Secretary, Highland Strathspey & Reel Society, 1936, page 1.

This letter to the society, dated 10 December 1913, is from Mr. William MacKay, Craigmonie, Inverness. Mr. Mackay has been asked to chair the forthcoming society annual concert in the Music Hall on 25 December. Unfortunately he is unable to attend as he has a prior engagement.

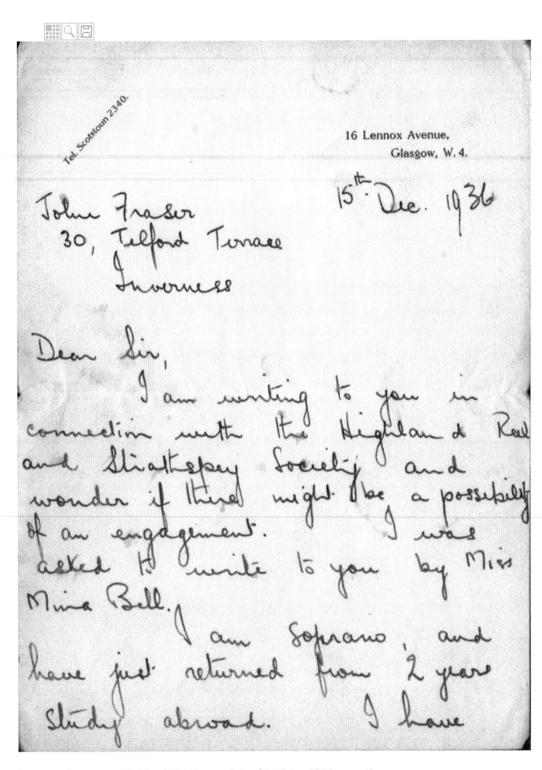

Tel. Scotstoun 2340.

16 Lennox Avenue,
Glasgow, W. 4.

John Fraser
30, Telford Terrace
Inverness

15th. Dec. 1936

Dear Sir,

I am writing to you in connection with the Highland Reel and Strathspey Society and wonder if there might be a possibility of an engagement. I was asked to write to you by Miss Mina Bell.

I am Soprano, and have just returned from 2 years study abroad. I have

Letter to Secretary, Highland Strathspey & Reel Society, 1936, page 1.

This letter (page 1) dated 15 December 1936 is from Joan Alexander, L.R.A.M., A.R.C.M., to the Highland branch Secretary, Mr. John Fraser. Miss Alexander is an experienced soprano singer. She asks to be considered for an engagement with the society and encloses critiques from a recent recital in Glasgow.

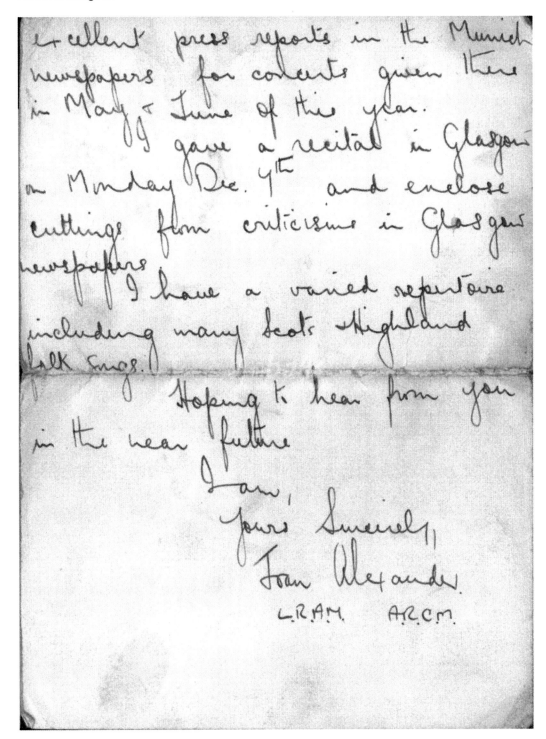

excellent press reports in the Munich newspapers for concerts given there in May & June of this year.

I gave a recital in Glasgow on Monday Dec. 4th and enclose cuttings from criticisms in Glasgow newspapers.

I have a varied repertoire including many Scots & Highland folk songs.

Hoping to hear from you in the near future

I am,

Yours Sincerely,

Joan Alexander.

L.R.A.M.   A.R.C.M.

Letter to Secretary, Highland Strathspey & Reel Society, 1936, page 2.

P.S. You'll have your Skinner grant from p.q. & now.

𝔥

12 Polmir Road,
~~37 Westburn Road,~~
Aberdeen.

16 · 11 · 86.

Dear Mrs Fraser,

Man, ye're a thorough chiel.
I admire you all the more for that.

You will see from your copy herewith
returned that "John Fraser" is a very flexible
reel. Although the set I gave you to present to
D. Morison is probably the set that will appear
in my next collection, 1960, the other set
is not unpleasant and may be preferred by some.
I have used pencil this time to distinguish one
grouping of notes from the other. The "D" you saw
in the original copy must have been an echo
of the later picture to be introduced in 5b.
If you can't follow me now, you'll have to
come along for a week's tuition!

I haven't heard yet how Patton and
MacPherson are taking to their latest treasures.
Tell them not to be so shy.

Regards in haste.

J. Murdoch Henderson

Letter to Secretary, Highland Strathspey & Reel Society, 16 Nov 1936.

142

This letter dated 16 November 1936 is from Jim Murdoch Henderson, Aberdeen, to the Highland branch Secretary, Mr. John Fraser. Mr. Henderson, himself a celebrated fiddler, composer and arranger, has recently sent three of his latest compositions; 'everlasting airs' specifically written for Mr. MacPherson, Mr. Fraser, and 'Battan' Grant. He asks how these compositions are being received.

19 Union Street

Inverness 3rd November 1936

Dear Sir,

Inverness Choral and Orchestral
Society

We propose holding our Annual
Scottish Concert in the Town Hall on
Monday 25th January 1937 and I should
like to know if The Highland Strathspey
and Reel Society will assist as usual
at the Concert. If they agree to do so,
I would like to get a list of the
selections they are to play. Two items –
one for each part of the programme.

An early reply will much oblige –

Yours sincerely

Archd MacGillivray
Hon Secy.

Letter to Secretary, Highland Strathspey & Reel Society, 3 Nov 1936.

This letter dated 3 November 1936 is from Archibald MacGillivray, Honorary Secretary of the Inverness Choral and Orchestral Society, to the Highland branch Secretary, Mr. John Fraser. Mr. MacGillivray requests that the Highland Strathspey and Reel Society assist at the forthcoming Annual Scottish Concert of the Choral Society.

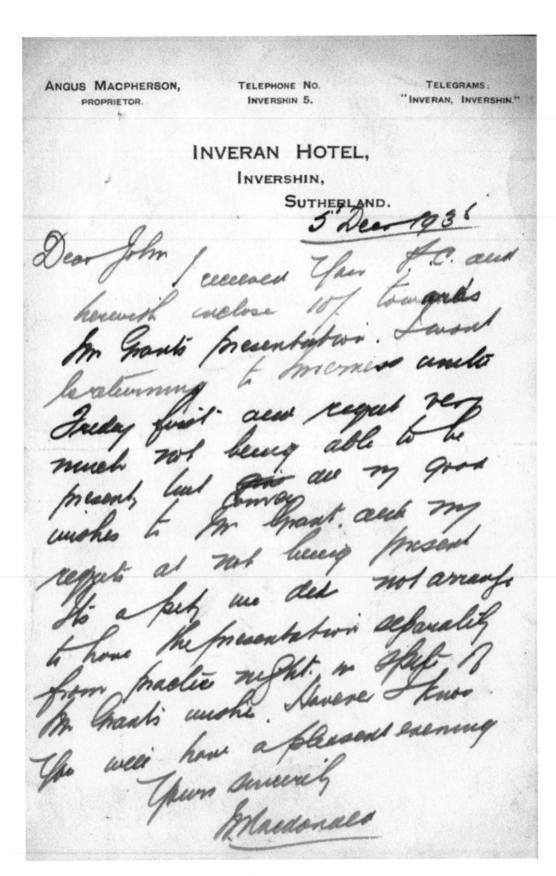

ANGUS MACPHERSON,
PROPRIETOR.

TELEPHONE NO.
INVERSHIN 5.

TELEGRAMS:
"INVERAN, INVERSHIN."

INVERAN HOTEL,
INVERSHIN,
SUTHERLAND.

5 Dec 1936

Dear John / received Your P.C. and herewith enclose 10/ towards Mr Grants presentation. I want to returning to Inverness until Friday first and regret very much not being able to be present, but you will convey all my good wishes to Mr Grant. and my regret at not being present. It's a pity we did not arrange to have the presentation separately from practice night, no efect, is Mr Grants wishes. I sincere I know you will have a pleasant evening

Yours sincerely,
E Macdonald

Letter to Secretary, Highland Strathspey & Reel Society, 5 Nov 1936.

This letter dated 5 November 1936 is from Mr. J. MacDonald (probably Pipe-Major John MacDonald) to the Highland branch Secretary, Mr. John Fraser. In it, Mr. MacDonald expresses his regret at being unable to attend a forthcoming presentation to Mr. Grant. He encloses ten shillings to put towards the event.

42 ROSS AVENUE,

INVERNESS.

10 - 11 - 36.

J. Fraser Esq,
Secretary,
Highland Strathspey & Reel Society.

Dear Mr Fraser.

I hasten to write to thank you most heartily for the gift of cigarettes which I received to day.

Please convey to your Society my most sincere thanks for such an acceptable present, and for the kind thoughts which prompted it.

Wishing you all success in the future.

Yours Sincerely,

J. MacKenzie.

Letter to Secretary, Highland Strathspey & Reel Society, 10 Nov 1936.

This letter dated 10 November 1936 is from Mr. J. MacKenzie, 42 Ross Avenue, Inverness, to the Highland branch Secretary, Mr. John Fraser. In it, Mr. MacKenzie expresses his gratitude for the gift of cigarettes he has recently received from the society.

Alexander 'Battan' Grant

1856 - 1942

(Fisherman, Musician & Fiddler of Note)

Part 3

Jock Scott – Grant's Fishing achievements and Rod Design

Alexander Grant and Gillie with the 55 lb salmon

caught on the river Garry in September 1887.

Fishing Acievements and Fame

There probably exists a considerable amount of printed material in past copies of the Fishing Gazette which mentions Alexander Grant by name, his engagement in debate with other fishermen on the pros and cons on fishing techniques, equipment, and lure fly's used in salmon fishing. One particular source which seems to be dispassionate and appears to give an accurate profile and description of the man's ability is the book published by Jock Scott (Donald Rudd):

Presented here are extracts from 'Fine and Far Off' by a leading fishing authority of the time *Jock Scott.

Book Dedication:

Dedicated to:

The memory of

ALEXANDER GRANT

The Wizard of the Ness

Who taught me many things.

There are numerous references to Mr Grant throughout this book to whom it is dedicated – here are quoted some of those. Bearing in mind the tense of the prose as was written at the time, for Mr Grant was still living when the book was being produced, but had died before the book went into print.

Preface:

My good friend, the late Mr. Alexander Grant, who inspired its writing, read this book in manuscript form and gave it his blessing. I did not then dream that I should be denied the great pleasure of presenting him with the finished volume, but fate intervened, and Mr Grant died at a very ripe old age of 86. If ever a man enjoyed his fishing he was that man. He was full of fun – teasing his companions, laughing at his and their misfortunes, and generally enjoying his day. The methods of fishing owe much to the teaching of other anglers, and chiefly to that of Mr Grant, one of the very greatest fly fishers of all time. The method first described, that originated by Mr Grant, will kill fish anywhere.

The Highlander is by nature a secretive man, and he does not willingly give away his hard-won knowledge; hence the fact that he suffers from lack of advertisement. 'Now I am not a Highlandman', and can therefore write without bias, and I feel sure that, were some of these men to journey south, they would set the Thames on fire just as Mr Grant did in 1895. They possess advantages which the southeron does not, because their rivers demand – in many cases – an extraordinary high standard of skill. Such streams as the Beauly, Ness, Spey and Findhorn are by no means child's play, compared to which the Tweed, Eden, Wye and Hampshire Avon are most easy to fish. To fish a pool from a plank situated at the foot of a vertical rock 80 feet high, down which one has scrambled with the aid of a wire rope, is not easy: neither is it easy to fish such a pool as the Rossie Lodge cast on the Ness, where a cast of at least 40 yards is needed to cover your fish, and where having fished out your cast, you have to lift your line from the clinging embrace of a most inconvenient slack. Or again, to tackle such a place as the Mare's Pool on the Beauly, casting into heavy water from the foot of a cliff, and throwing at least 35 to 40 yards to cover certain lies, is a far sterner form of fishing than the south provides.

Seriously speaking, the two fishing worlds – north and south – are poles apart. It is true that the southerner takes his technique to the far north, but he is merely a visitor, and I speak of the native practitioner, Alexander Grant, a native of the Spey valley, afterwards transplanted to the Ness, is as different from the average Wye angler, for example, as chalk from cheese.

Perhaps it is unfortunate that Mr. Grant's name and methods are most frequently associated with record casts, and controversy thereon. The value of his method lies, to my mind, in the fact that the ordinary mortal may make casts of tournament length under actual fishing conditions, if required. What he himself has done in the past merely serves to show what can be done, and what he did was far more than is needed under fishing conditions – maybe 20 yards or more – for he has actually cast a fly 60 yards. However, while such colossal casts may be done under favourable circumstances, they are exceptional; ***but I should like to emphasis the fact that he habitually – not occasionally – hooked and killed fish at from 40 to 50 yards range.*** He deliberately, and from choice, approached fish from that distance, and his long list of catches, ranging from 6 lb. grilse to a salmon of 55 lb. from the Garry, proves that he was working on sound lines.

I know that casting records are, to his mind, merely incidental; his idea was to evolve a fishing method pure and simple, and that his actual fishing gear – not special tools – made such astonishing casts simply proved the efficiency thereof. Once, and once only, did I persuade him to go really all out, and the length of line he could throw at the age of 79 was unbelievable, and this was the rod which he had been using to catch fish.

Mr Grant is a lightning fisher; he never wastes time and does not believe in bullying – or trying to bully – a fish into taking. "He'll come if he's coming at all". Three times over a fish and then leave him is about the limit of Mr Grant' attentions.

I have been a friend of Mr Grant's for quite a number of years, we have fished together almost every summer, we have argued, agreed, disagreed, and even abused each other, and still remain friends. He is a genial autocrat on his own subject and many a time have I attempted to lay snares for his unwary feet, but without success. I do not think I have ever met a man with so complete a knowledge of his particular line, or one more ready to produce a convincing reason for his actions. It is a mark of the extraordinary thoroughness with which all his ideas are worked out that, try which way you may, you can never succeed in extracting any conflicting statement. That is the result of the scientific mind applied to fishing, for Mr Grant is a scientist. Accustomed to scientific and deadly accuracy he insists on its application to his sport. The result was that, when he was teaching me to cast, he insisted on perfection, and his lurid description of what I thought was quite good casting still lingers in my memory. With Mr Grant there is no such thing as being "quite good" – either you are "good", which to him means perfect, or "no d...d good at all". His motto is, "either a thing is right or it isn't, and if it isn't, it's not worth troubling about". Similarly, "Why" he said, "take any trouble at all unless you are going to take enough? An imperfect job is no use to anyone".

Probably as a result of his love of accuracy for accuracy's sake, Mr Grant has few fishing stories to tell. One would imagine that a man of 83 would, out of his lifelong experience, have some tales to tell; but I have only once succeeded in extracting a fishing story of the usual kind – it refers to the fish which got away. The incident occurred during the last century, and some time after the capture of the 55 lb. fish previously mentioned. Mr Grant hooked a great salmon, with which he could do absolutely nothing. He asserts that this fish was far heavier than the 55- pounder. The water was up and he was using a 17-foot rod and heavy gut, which he put to the utmost limit of their power; in fact, he held so hard as to pull all the spring out of the rod – no easy feat – and yet made no impression whatever. At long last the hold gave and what he describes as the greatest salmon he ever saw was free. Mr Grant has had too much experience to make mistakes over the size of a fish, either in or out of the water, and when he classes this salmon as being between 60 and 70 lb. I believe him.

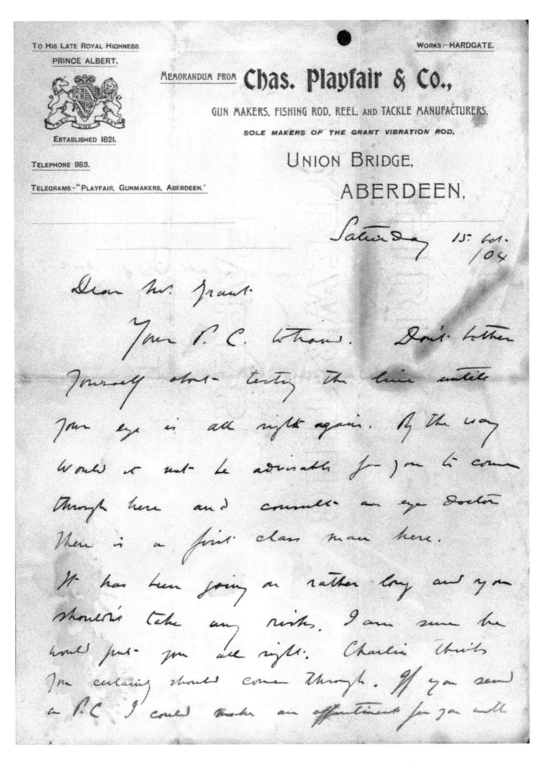

Memo from Chas. Playfair & Co. to Alexander Grant, 1904 (front).

In the early 1900s, Grant sold the patent rights to his 'Vibration Rods' to Charles Playfair & Co., fishing tackle makers in Aberdeen. This memo to Grant dated 15 October 1904 is from John Roll of Playfairs. In it, Mr. Roll refers to Mr. Grant's recent eye complaint and urges him to come through to Aberdeen to visit a 'first class' doctor. Mr. Charles Playfair is of the same opinion.

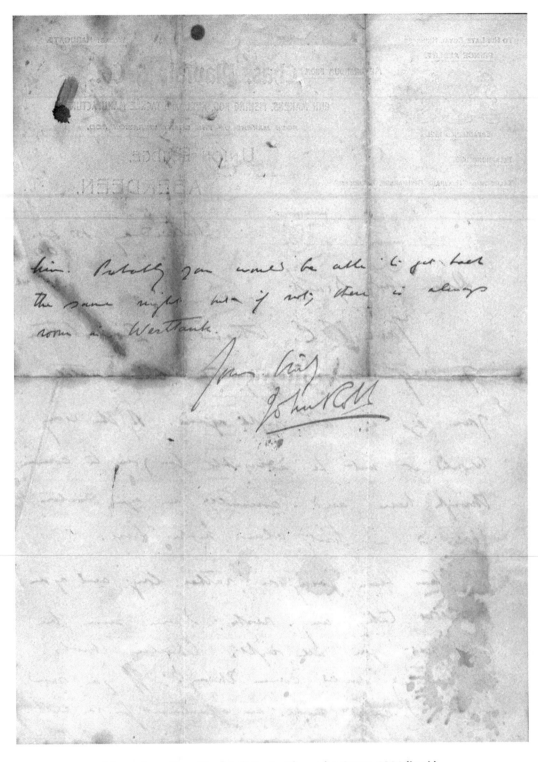

him. Probably you would be able to get back the same night but if not; there is always room in WestTank.

Yours truly
John ...

Memo from Chas. Playfair & Co. to Alexander Grant, 1904 (back).

Offices for Patents and the Registration of Designs and Trade Marks.

MESS^{RS} JOHNSONS.

115 St Vincent Street,
Glasgow, 15th May 1900

Renewal of British Patent
N° 10385 of 29th May 1894

Dear Sir,

We beg to request that you will now favour us by payment of Account rendered, on before 22nd inst.
Amount £ 8 : 1 : 0

We are, Dear Sir
Yours truly,
Johnsons
P.W.

Alex. Grant Esq,
Inverness.

Grant's Vibration Rod - Patent Registration Renewal, May 1900.

Grant patented his 'Vibration Rod' in 1894. This letter to Grant, dated 15 May 1900, is from Messrs Johnsons, 115 St. Vincent Street, Glasgow (Offices for Patents and the Registration of Designs and Trade Marks). The letter requests payment of £8 1s 0d for renewal of the British patent No. 10385.

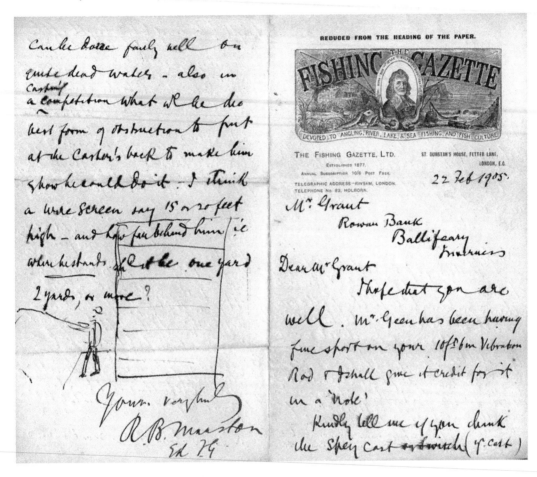

Letter to Alexander Grant (Battan) from 'The Fishing Gazette', 1905.

This letter to Grant dated 22 February 1905 is from the editor of the 'Fishing Gazette'. In it, he asks Grant's advice on some technical questions concerning fly casting and competitions.

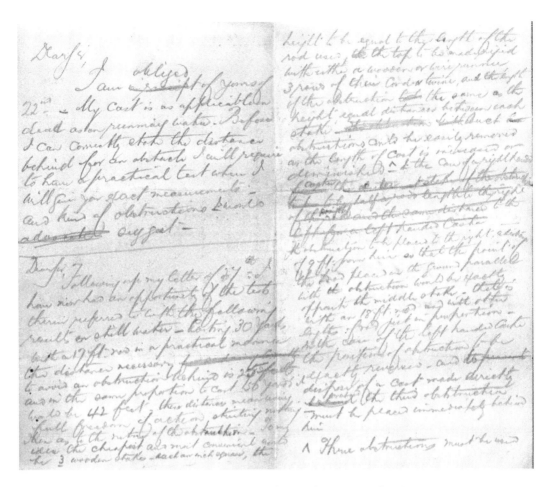

Draft Letter from Grant to 'The Fishing Gazette', 1905.

On 22 February 1905 the editor of the 'Fishing Gazette' wrote to Grant asking his advice on some technical questions concerning fly casting and competitions. On the reverse of the letter (pictured here) Grant appears to have drafted his reply in pencil.

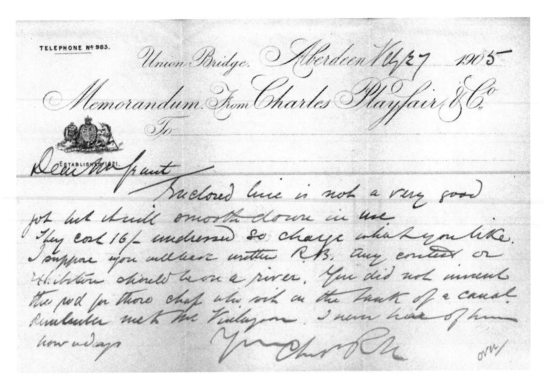

Memo to Grant from Charles Playfair & Co., 1905, (front).

Grant patented his 'Vibration Rod' in 1894. In the early 1900s he sold the patent rights to Charles Playfair & Co., fishing tackle makers in Aberdeen. This memo to Grant, dated 27 February 1905, is from Charles Playfair. It accompanied a consignment of rods which, in Playfair's words are 'not a very good job' but 'will smooth down in use'. The rods cost sixteen shillings undressed and Playfair instructs Grant to 'charge what you like'. On the back of the memo, Mr. Playfair mentions a Mr. Newlands.

N° 10,385  A.D. 1894

Date of Application, 28th May, 1894
Complete Specification Left, 24th Jan., 1895—Accepted, 4th May, 1895

PROVISIONAL SPECIFICATION.

A Non-slipping Splice for Fishing Rods, Golf Club Handles, and other like Articles.

I, ALEXANDER GRANT, of 7 Baron Taylor's Lane, in the Town and County of Inverness, North Britain, Fishing Rod and Tackle Maker, do hereby declare the nature of this invention to be as follows :—

This invention relates to a non-slipping splice for fishing rods, golf club handles,
5 and other like articles, and has for its object to provide a splice which wont slip and which whether tied or untied is stronger than the ordinary splice and it is easier fitted & tied.

In constructing the splice, preparation is made for it from the commencement of the work. The wood is first squared, the part for the splice made with an upward
10 or downward slope as the case may be, then the shaft or handle is rounded off to the inner end of splice leaving the part to be spliced square or flat. The splices are then shaped & made. To make a splice of the same pattern but not so complete in details, the wood is rounded altogether making the part to be spliced with a bend upwards or downwards, as before, but it cannot fit accurately as the
15 shoulders will be wanting at the inner end of the splice. These shoulders are taken away by the rounding of the stick at the beginning.

The splices are sloped against each other so that the rod or other article made will come out straight at each end of the splice, or in other words the connection is running direct.
20 All vibrating articles naturally made may be balanced before the splice is interfered with.

Dated this 28th day of May 1894.

JOHNSONS,
115, St. Vincent Street, Glasgow, Applicant's Agents

25 COMPLETE SPECIFICATION.

A Non-slipping Splice for Fishing Rods, Golf Club Handles, and other like Articles.

I, ALEXANDER GRANT, of 7 Baron Taylor's Lane, in the Town and County of Inverness, North Britain Fishing Rod and Tackle Maker, do hereby declare the
30 nature of this invention and in what manner the same is to be performed, to be particularly described and ascertained in and by the following statement :—

This invention relates to a non-slipping splice for fishing rods, golf club handles, and other like articles, and has for its object to provide a splice which will not slip and which whether tied or untied is stronger than the ordinary splice, and also a
35 splice which can be fitted and tied much easier than hitherto.

In carrying out my said invention as illustrated in elevation Figure 1 and sectional under plan Figure 2, of the accompanying drawings, I construct the splice in the following manner :—The wood is first squared, then the parts to be joined are made with an upward or downward slope bend or half splice (as the

[Price 8d.]

Patent Specification for Grant's 'Non-slipping Splice', page 1.

Grant applied for a patent on his invention - officially called 'A Non-slipping Splice for Fishing Rods, Golf Club Handles, and other like Articles' - on 29 May 1894. It was accepted on 4 May 1895. This is page one of the Patent Specification issued by Johnsons Patent Office, 115 St. Vincent Street, Glasgow. It gives a detailed description of the invention.

Grant's Non-slipping Splice for Fishing Rods, Golf Club Handles, &c.

case may be) so as to ensure of the centres being in line and so secure direct action ; then the shaft or handle is rounded off to the inner end of the splices A, A¹, so as to form shoulders a, a^1, leaving the part to be spliced square or flat. The splices or flat portions are then secured together by tying or otherwise, so as to construct a very efficient non-slipping splice.   5

As a modification I may round the wood of the handle altogether making the part to be spliced with a bend upwards or downwards, as before, but this form lacks the power and does not fit so accurately when the shoulders are wanting at the inner end of the splice. These shoulders are taken away by the rounding of the stick at the beginning.   10

It will be seen that on the sloped or flat portions A, A¹, being placed against each other, the rod or other article made will come out straight at each end of the splice, as shewn, or in other words the connection is running direct.

Having now particularly described and ascertained the nature of my said invention, and in what manner the same is to be performed, I declare that what I   15 claim is :—

The arrangement and construction of the non-slipping splice, for fishing rods and the like, substantially as and for the purposes hereinbefore described and shewn in the accompanying drawings.

Dated this 23rd day of January 1895.   20

JOHNSONS,
115, St. Vincent Street, Glasgow, Applicant's Agents.

London : Printed for Her Majesty's Stationery Office, by Darling & Son, Ltd.—1895

Patent Specification for Grant's 'Non-slipping Splice', page 2.

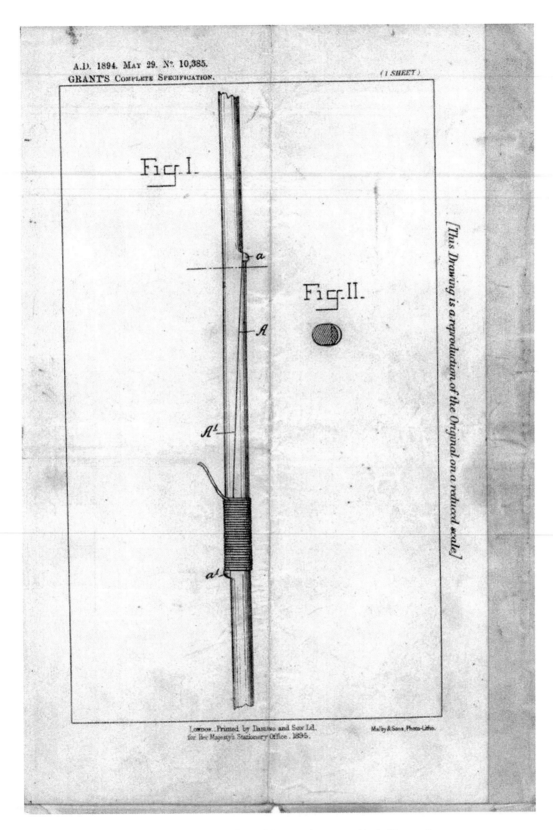

Patent Specification for Grant's 'Non-slipping Splice', illustration.

Grant applied for a patent on his invention - officially called 'A Non-slipping Splice for Fishing Rods, Golf Club Handles, and other like Articles' - on 29 May 1894. It was accepted on 4 May 1895. This is the illustration which accompanied the Patent Specifications issued by Johnsons Patent Office, 115 St. Vincent Street, Glasgow. It shows a detailed, scaled-down drawing of the splice.

Patent Specification for Grant's 'Non-slipping Splice', illustration.

This memo dated 25 August 1898 is from Grant to a prospective customer in Tettenhall, Wolverhampton. In it, Grant details the merits of his 'Vibration Rod' and refers the gentleman to an article in the periodical 'Land and Water', 19th December 1896.

Letter from Alexander Grant to J. B. Dunning, 7 Apr 1893, page 1.

This letter (draft?) dated 7 April 1893 is from Grant to a Mr. J. B. Dunning. In it Grant informs Mr. Dunning that his recently ordered fishing rod is complete, apart from 'rings and fittings' (newly invented by Grant and awaiting patent registration). Once the parts arrive from the Birmingham manufacturers, Grant will forward the completed rod forthwith. In addition, Grant advises of his letter in last week's issue of 'Land and Water', under the heading, 'Fly Rods for Trout Fishing'.

7 Baron Taylors Lane
Inverness
3rd Feb. 1894

My dear Sir,

I have no time just now to write you fully in reference to Casting competitions as my principle man is laid up, but I have noted below a few points on the subject which you can alter & amend at your discretion.

The manner in which casting competitions are presently conducted is I consider unsatisfactory to practical fishers. To allow the competitor to stand on an elevated platform or barge with an open space behind & only testing them on one point & proficiency on one

Letter from Alexander Grant, 3 Feb 1894, page 1.

In May 1887 Grant moved his fishing rod and tackle business from Carrbridge to Inverness, initially at Glenalbyn Buildings, Young Street. He later moved to premises at 7 Baron Taylor's Lane, from where this (draft?) letter was written on 3 February 1894. The intended recipient is unknown but it may be a fellow angler or editor of a contemporary angling publication as Grant invites him to 'alter & amend' the letter as he sees fit. The bulk of the letter is taken up with Grant's opinions on current fly casting competitions which he finds 'unsatisfactory to practical fishers'.

Letter from Alexander Grant, 3 Feb 1894, pages 2 & 3.

with the first prize.

The Casting Competitions should
be held on water where obstacles
exist, or if not obstacles should be
constructed, as far as possible
to bring out the various ways
of casting. Thin pointed stakes
wd do if better it not be fat
and close ed be stuck in the
ground as near the fisher as
possible without interfering
with the action of the rod.
but in a manner that wd
make his over head cast an
impossibility. of course the over
head or shoulder cast wd have
a place in the competitions
though it is the most elementary
& easiest cast of the practical
anglers methods. A competition
such as I suggest would be
more difficult to carry out &
would require competent judges

Letter from Alexander Grant, 3 Feb 1894, page 4.

but surely it is quite
apparent that the result wd
be far more satisfactory
to all concerned than the
incomplete & one sided
manner in which our
present competitions are
planned conducted & decided,

You can do with this letter
what you like & if you are
afraid to put your own
name to it put "Rattanyani"
In any case you must
rely on yourself for the con-
tinuance of the correspondence
which you are so well able
to do as I cannot be
bothered with, such in
the meantime. If you

are going to make this rise with the bay line
a continuation of your
former letter you ed
head it. The art of Casting
and Casting Competitions.
This will let the readers see
that you have again
written as you promised
as perhaps you may
not have occasion to
add any more for some
time and if you should
happen to want help
in future call on
"Mr Hardy" as I am
not in. Perhaps Mr
Hardy will show you how
to hit a fish on the

Letter from Alexander Grant, 3 Feb 1894, pages 6 & 7.

Offices for Patents and the Registration of Designs and Trade Marks.

MESS^{RS} JOHNSONS,

115, St Vincent Street,

Glasgow, 23rd May 1899

Alex Grant Esqr

Inverness,

Dear Sir,

We beg to acknowledge receipt of your _____ Cheque _____ for £ 7 . 1 . 0 _____ in settlement of above accompanying a/c.

We are much obliged to you for same and beg to enclose our receipt herewith.

We are,

Yours faithfully,

Johnsons

James L. Wells

2 Enclosures

Grant's Vibration Rod - Patent Registration Receipt, 1899.

Grant patented his 'Vibration Rod' in 1894. This letter to Grant, dated 23 May 1899, is from Messrs Johnsons, 115 St. Vincent Street, Glasgow (Offices for Patents and the Registration of Designs and Trade Marks). The letter acknowledges receipt of Grant's cheque for £7 1s 0d in settlement of tax and agency fees due on the patent renewal.

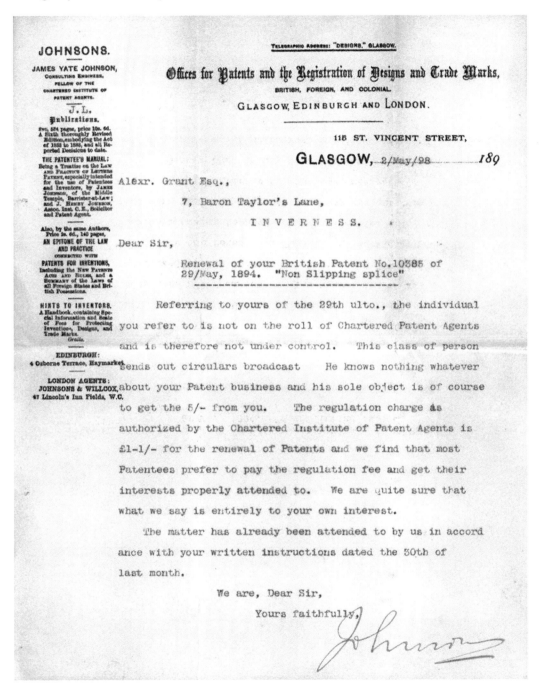

Letter to Grant from Messrs Johnsons, Patent Agents, 2 May 1898.

Grant patented his 'Vibration Rod' on 29 May 1894. This letter to Grant, dated 2 May 1898, is from Messrs Johnsons, 115 St. Vincent Street, Glasgow (Offices for Patents and the Registration of

Designs and Trade Marks). In the letter, the agents confirm certain actions taken by them, on behalf of Mr. Grant, regarding patent regulations and charges.

JOHNSONS.

JAMES YATE JOHNSON,
CONSULTING ENGINEER,
FELLOW OF THE
CHARTERED INSTITUTE OF
PATENT AGENTS.

J.L.
Publications.

8vo, 584 pages, price 10s. 6d.
A Sixth thoroughly Revised
Edition, embodying the Act
of 1883 to 1886, and all Reported Decisions to date.

THE PATENTEE'S MANUAL;
Being a Treatise on the Law
AND PRACTICE OF LETTERS
PATENT, especially intended
for the use of Patentees
and Inventors, by JAMES
JOHNSON, of the Middle
Temple, Barrister-at-Law;
and J. HENRY JOHNSON,
Assoc. Inst. C.E., Solicitor
and Patent Agent.

Also, by the same Authors,
Price 2s. 6d., 140 pages,
AN EPITOME OF THE LAW
AND PRACTICE
CONNECTED WITH
PATENTS FOR INVENTIONS,
Including the New Patents
ACTS AND RULES, and a
SUMMARY of the Laws of
all Foreign States and Bri-
tish Possessions.

HINTS TO INVENTORS.
A Handbook, containing Spe-
cial Information and Scale
of Fees for Protecting
Inventions, Designs, and
Trade Marks.
Gratis.

EDINBURGH:
4 Osborne Terrace, Haymarket.

LONDON AGENTS:
JOHNSONS & WILLCOX,
47 Lincoln's Inn Fields, W.C.

TELEGRAPHIC ADDRESS: "DESIGNS." GLASGOW.

Offices for Patents and the Registration of Designs and Trade Marks,

BRITISH, FOREIGN, AND COLONIAL.

GLASGOW, EDINBURGH AND LONDON.

115 ST. VINCENT STREET,

GLASGOW, 6/May/98 189

Alexr. Grant Esq.,

I N V E R N E S S.

Dear Sir,

Your British Patent No.10385 /94.

As instructed in yours of the 25th ulto.,
we beg to enclose Official certificate of the renewal of
the above for a further period of one year.

We beg also to enclose our a/c.

We are, Dear Sir,

Yours faithfully,

Johnsons Jw.

Enclosure.
Official certificate.
A/c.

Letter to Grant from Messrs Johnsons, Patent Agents, 6 May 1898.

Grant patented his 'Vibration Rod' on 29 May 1894 - No. 10385. This letter to Grant, dated 6 May 1898, is from Messrs Johnsons, 115 St. Vincent Street, Glasgow (Offices for Patents and the

Registration of Designs and Trade Marks). The letter confirms renewal of the patent for a further year.

Messrs. Innes & Mackay
Inverness.

Dear Sirs,   Grants Registered Design
We duly received yours of the 22nd inst.—
The marking can be put upon keeper
perfectly well; it does not in the least matter if
the marking is hidden.—

We are, Dear Sirs
Yours faithfully
Johnsons

Letter to Innes & Mackay from Johnsons, Patent Agents, 25 May 1898.

Grant patented his 'Vibration Rod' on 29 May 1894 - No. 10385. This letter to Messrs. Innes & Mackay (solicitors) Inverness, dated 25 May 1898, is from Messrs. Johnsons, 115 St. Vincent Street,

Glasgow (Offices for Patents and the Registration of Designs and Trade Marks). It refers to a particular 'marking' issue.

Letter to Grant from Messrs Johnsons, Patent Agents, 23 Mar 1899.

Grant patented his 'Vibration Rod' on 29 May 1894 - No. 10385. This letter to Grant, dated 23 March 1899, is from Messrs Johnsons, 115 St. Vincent Street, Glasgow (Offices for Patents and the

Registration of Designs and Trade Marks). It is a reminder for tax and agency fees due on the patent renewal - an amount of £7 1s 0d.

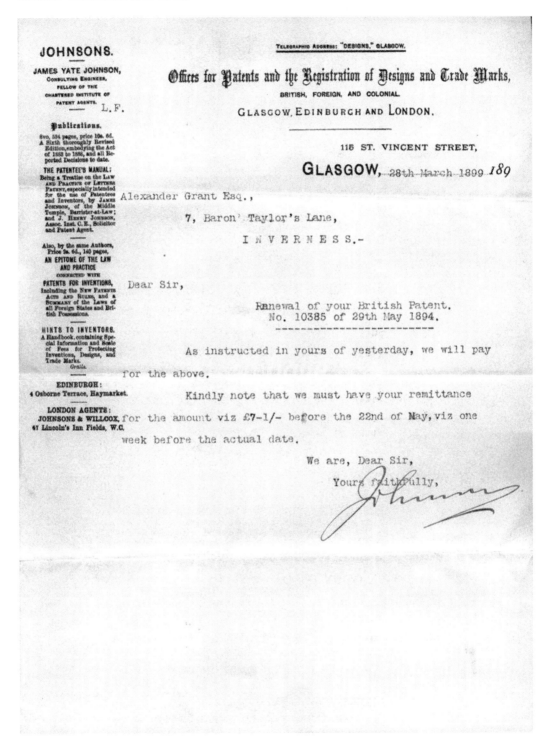

Letter to Grant from Messrs Johnsons, Patent Agents, 28 Mar 1899.

Grant patented his 'Vibration Rod' on 29 May 1894 - No. 10385. This letter to Grant, dated 28 March 1899, is from Messrs Johnsons, 115 St. Vincent Street, Glasgow (Offices for Patents and the

Registration of Designs and Trade Marks). It is a request for payment for the patent renewal for a further year.

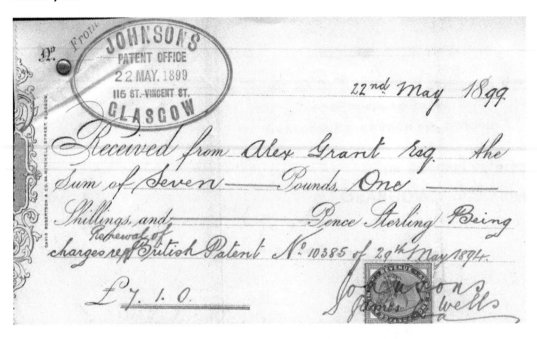

Receipt to Grant from Messrs Johnsons, Patent Agents, 22 May 1899.

Grant patented his 'Vibration Rod' on 29 May 1894 - No. 10385. This receipt, dated 22 May 1899, is from Messrs Johnsons, 115 St. Vincent Street, Glasgow (Offices for Patents and the Registration of Designs and Trade Marks). It acknowledges receipt of amount due for patent renewal for a further year - a charge of £7 1s 0d.

TELEPHONE No. 5726.   TELEGRAPHIC ADDRESS: "DESIGNS." GLASGOW.

NSONS.

Offices for Patents and the Registration of Designs and Trade Marks,

BRITISH, FOREIGN, AND COLONIAL.

GLASGOW, EDINBURGH AND LONDON.

115 ST. VINCENT STREET,

GLASGOW, 15th May 1899.

Alexr. Grant Esq,
            Inverness,

_____ to _____

Johnsons

To charges re Renewal of your British
Patent No. 10385 of 29th May 1894 for
a further period of one year.—   £7. 1. 0

Cheque £7. 1/- Stg. enclosed, as requested—
                p/C. Grant,
                        J.J.

Kindly let us have your cheque.

Invoice to Grant from Messrs Johnsons, Patent Agents, 15 May 1899.

Grant patented his 'Vibration Rod' on 29 May 1894 - No. 10385. This invoice, dated 15 May 1899, is from Messrs Johnsons, 115 St. Vincent Street, Glasgow (Offices for Patents and the Registration of Designs and Trade Marks). The charge of £7 1s 0d is for the patent renewal for a further year. Mr. Grant has signed and returned the invoice with his payment.

7 Baron Taylors Lane
Inverness 9th Feby 93

Sir

I am favoured with your letter of 3rd inst. for which I am obliged.

My price for an 18 ft. rod made of washaba (which is the wood referred to by Mr. Corballis) in three pieces, with spliced joints, and three tops, would ~~any~~ range from £7..7/. to £10..10/. according to the quality of the wood used.

I do not now on any account make rods with socket joints or with upright

Letter to R. R. Herbert, France, from Alexander Grant, 1893, page 1.

Grant moved to Inverness in 1887 to start up a fishing rod and tackle business in Baron Taylor's Lane. At the back of his premises was a hairdressing shop. This copy letter (dated 9 February 1893) was written while Grant was at Baron Taylor's Lane. It is a reply to an enquiry from 'R. R. Fitz Herbert Esq.', Biarritz, France. The letter includes information on the construction, price and estimated delivery of Grant's fishing rods.

ings, as my experience convinces me of their inefficacy.

The principle on which I make my rods though new in practice is old as the world itself, as it is a natural principle and is the only method of making them complete in themselves, the sending power and strength being in accordance with the quality of the material used.

For fly rods I use rings invented by myself which are specially adapted to the principle on which the rods are made.

I usually make my rods in two pieces with one splice, but I have often made them in three pieces, with two splices, in which form they are equally good, more portable and durable and in case of accident more easily repaired

Should you favour me with an order for a Sal rod made as I have indicated I shall endeavour to have it completed in all respects first class

Letter to R. R. Herbert, France, from Alexander Grant, 1893, pages 2 & 3.

within four months
time

I am Sir
Your obedient Servant
Alex Grant.

R. R. Fitz Herbert Esq
Maison Trois
Biarritz
France.

Letter to R. R. Herbert, France, from Alexander Grant, 1893, page 4.

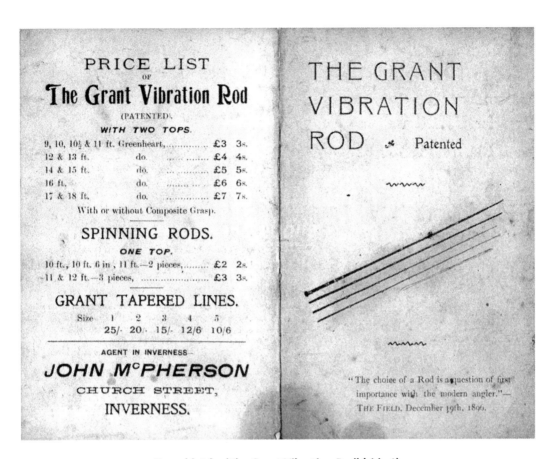

PRICE LIST

OF

The Grant Vibration Rod

(PATENTED).

WITH TWO TOPS.

9, 10, 10½ & 11 ft. Greenheart,.............. £3 3s.
12 & 13 ft.   do.   .... £4 4s.
14 & 15 ft.   do.   .... £5 5s.
16 ft.   do.   .... £6 6s.
17 & 18 ft.   do.   .... £7 7s.

With or without Composite Grasp.

SPINNING RODS.

ONE TOP.

10 ft., 10 ft. 6 in., 11 ft.—2 pieces,......... £2 2s.
11 & 12 ft.—3 pieces, ... £3 3s.

GRANT TAPERED LINES.

Size	1	2	3	4	5
	25/-	20/-	15/-	12/6	10/6

AGENT IN INVERNESS—

JOHN M°PHERSON

CHURCH STREET,

INVERNESS.

**THE GRANT
VIBRATION
ROD** ✤ Patented

"The choice of a Rod is a question of first
importance with the modern angler."—
THE FIELD. December 19th. 1896.

Pamphlet for 'The Grant Vibration Rod' (side 1).

In the early 1900s, Grant sold the patent rights to his 'Vibration Rods' to Charles Playfair & Co., fishing tackle makers in Aberdeen. This pamphlet (side 1) lists prices for the rods. The Inverness agent at this time was John McPherson, Church Street.

REASONS

for USING the

GRANT ROD

It has more lifting and driving power than any other.

o o o

It is practically unbreakable.

o o o

It is easier to fish with, and saves the Angler's strength.

o o o

The balance is perfect.

OPINIONS.

ROTHIEMAY, Oct., 1909.

"I find the 17 ft. a beauty."—C. I.

RICHMOND, 2nd March, 1908.

"They are the best rods he has ever used."—Z.

DORNOCH, 30th Aug., 1909.

"They admitted unanimously its superiority in every respect; but most especially in the superadded elasticity gained by abolition of the metal fixings."
—W. S. N. D. S. O.

GLASGOW, 28th May, 1909.

"I found it much lighter and better balanced than an expensive double built cane rod, steel centre of same length."
—J. H. C.

WOLVERHAMPTON, 13th Aug., 1909.

"I can say with safety that I have never had a rod of equal weight with which I can lift such a length of line."
—H G. D.

For other Testimonials see Pamphlet. Originals can be seen at

PLAYFAIR & CO.,

Union Bridge, ABERDEEN.

Pamphlet for 'The Grant Vibration Rod' (side 2).

Grant patented his 'Vibration Rod' in 1894. In the early 1900s he sold the patent rights to Charles Playfair & Co., fishing tackle makers in Aberdeen. This pamphlet (side 2) lists reasons for using the Grant rod together with several short testimonials.

Sir/ Kindly allow me to correct the following printers error in my letter to your paper, which appeared on May 17th. Your print. "If made a little off the principle &c.' Which should be "if made a title off the principle" &c the term in this case being important.

Allow me also to endorse your opinion that "it it will never do to claim perfection for the rod which makes the longest cast" & term I have always advocated, vide "Rod &c of Nov the 28d 1895 &c. At the same time a perfect rod shd possess the greatest power of its weight. If my rods were not able to show superiority in this respect what av_ he said, I am opposed & have always been to casting that is not of a practical character & adaptable under all

This draft letter (undated) was written by Grant and is on the subject of fly casting. It has been written on the back of a poster for the 'Railway Watch Company's Prize Draw' (July 1900). The intended recipient is the editor of a paper or periodical in which a previous letter of Grant's has recently appeared. Grant covers several issues in this letter including a printing error made in his last letter; his opposition to overhead casting and shooting of lines; his casting exhibition on the River Thames; and the benefits of his 'Vibration Rod'.

circumstances; i.e. any position a fisher may happen to find himself in. ¹ The cast you refer to as a record one I made to demonstrate this. Over head casting & shooting of lines, I hold to be un practical & opposed to the true art of fishing. "The ~~power of my rods, on lifting a line~~ power of my rods I also demonstrated at the casting ex-hibitions on the Thames, when I contended that if a rod cast 50 y<u>ds</u> practically as above, it shd lift "70 <u>yds</u> (or 20 y<u>ds</u> more) & thus with a fishing rod & line as used in <u>fishing</u>. As facts alone are admissable here. I quote Litw of Dec 19<u>th</u> 1896 which says.

"One of Mr Grants assertions is that a rod capable of casting fifty y^ds on water she lift twenty y^ds more on dry land, and this test, not as any angling ~~test~~ but as a lifting test, he tried on the grass. The line was run out &c the reel & then cast over head. In this manner Mr S cast 74 y^ds, or, in point of fact every inch there was on the reel & the line fell dead true. The rod measured 18ft 5in."

"This you will observe was with an overhead cast. The cast of 53 y^ds quoted by you was done in the practical method (or what I term the Planet Cast) referred to which shews I am only concerned about practical results. It shows nevertheless the Grant. V.R. is able under a system of fishing which I regard as impractical to do the work in that manner as no other rod does,

In short the rod is fit for its work & does not depend on the mere force which can be applied

Draft Letter (undated) from Alexander Grant, page 3.

188

This Demonstrated, on the Shumas

The lifting power of my rods I also demonstrated when an 18 ... gas
of line.

Draft Letter (undated) from Alexander Grant, page 4.

RAILWAY WATCH COMPANY'S
GRAND PRIZE DRAWING

WILL now take place without fail on TUESDAY, the 10th of JULY, 1900. Agents will please make sure that all Duplicates are returned in time, otherwise they will be debarred from participating in the Drawing.

200 PRIZES,
Amounting to £280,
Now on View in our Windows.

Tickets, Sixpence each.

One Ticket given with every Sixpence worth of purchases.

RAILWAY WATCH COMPANY,
18 New Market Buildings,

JULY, 1900.

Draft Letter (undated) from Alexander Grant, page 5.

ALEXANDER GRANT

❊ Fishing=Rod and Tackle Maker ❊

BEGS to intimate that he has REMOVED from CARR-BRIDGE
to the Shop

GLENALBYN BUILDINGS, YOUNG STREET

INVERNESS

Where he is now prepared to execute all Orders with which he
may be favoured.

Being a thoroughly practical Fisherman, he is able to supply
Rods and Flies of his own make—a business in which he has been
steadily acquiring a knowledge from his earlier years—of the very
best material; and as to exactness of finish equal to any in the
trade.

Rods made to Order or Repaired on the shortest notice, at Moderate
Charges, and Flies Dressed to any Pattern or description, and
supplied to suit the Scotch Rivers and Lochs.

---

*Letters of approval from Anglers on the Tweed, Tay, Spey, &c.,
may be perused at the Shop by intending purchasers.*

INVERNESS, *26th May 1887.*

Alexander Grant's Change of Address Notification, 26 May 1887.

In May 1887 Grant moved his fishing rod and tackle business from Carrbridge to Inverness, initially at Glenalbyn Buildings, Young Street. He later moved to premises at 7 Baron Taylor's Lane. This change of address notification dates from his first move to Inverness.

'Grant's Vibration Rod' - Letter (no date), page 1.

This letter, possibly a draft, was written by Grant and relates to the supply of his 'Vibration Rods'. Although undated, it was written after he patented the design in 1894. The intended recipient is unknown, but Grant refers to a Mr. Corballis (Inverness magistrate and angling author) who has asked Grant to send a rod to the recipient. Due to the increased demand for his product, Grant is unable to fulfil Mr. Corballis's request; he works 'unaided' as he is 'reluctant to divulge the secret' of the rods' construction.

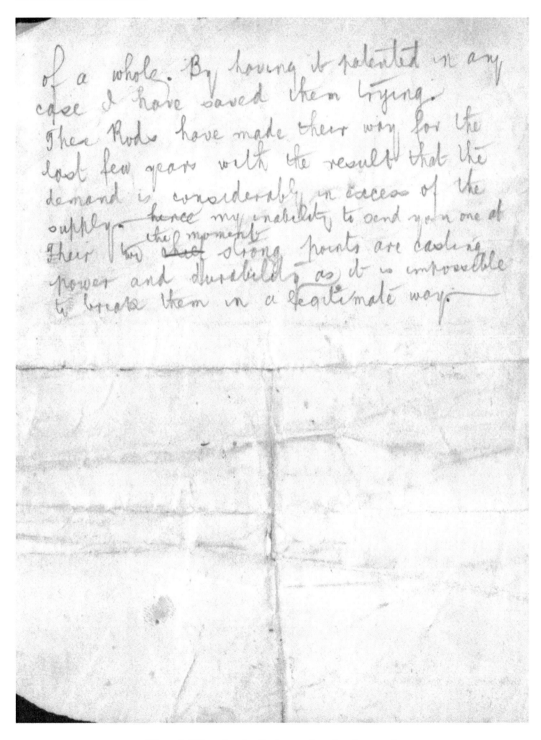

'Grant's Vibration Rod' - Letter (no date), page 2.

Col Bennet

My dear Sir'

I have to thank you for your very interesting letter only to hand re-dressing for lines. In the first place I do not care for any mixtures ~~& he~~ I have invariably tried conservations including most of the substances you refer to & had to discard all ~~of them~~ except boiled linseed any of the substances you mention added to the boiled tends to harden ~~that is supposed to~~ free a line & you quite understand that any ingredient added to harden wont do, therefore use only linseed ~~&~~ & to do up the part needed to be done, do it in this way fill a pint or ½ pint of boiled linseed empty the contents into a 2 or 4d treacle tin then boil your line or part thereof in the tins until oil leaving it there

Grant's Headed Accounts Sheet, Ballifeary Post Office (back).

Grant had a varied career working at various times as a shepherd, ploughman, draper, forester, grocer, butcher, gamekeeper, fisherman, hairdresser and fishing tackle merchant. This headed accounts sheet (back) is for Grant's grocery and post office at Ballifeary, Inverness. Grant has used the sheet to draft a letter in reply to a query from a fellow angler.

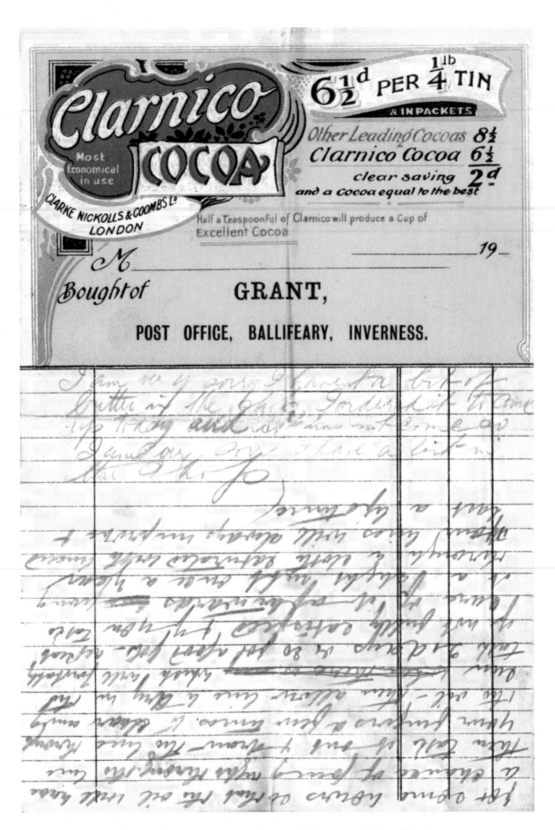

Grant's Headed Accounts Sheet, Ballifeary Post Office (front).

I did not mean that the new line w^d be
tapered to a finer point than ~~that it~~ ^that one
is as you have it, because as it is ~~it is~~ it is
drawn.
fine enough for a single Sal cast &
a No 2 or 3 Sal fly – the finer bit can
always be added or taken away as desired
for ^now Competition or exhibition purposes.
I am very glad you have ~~more~~ one ~~will~~ ^the better
idea for the making of ^the Rod ~~It you any~~
~~the from the beginning~~ ^from your description
however make it ^the taper ^you made
can ^be ~~not~~ correct – too level or long. I sh^d say
you w^d require to take out a ~~thread~~ every
half y^d ^in your ~~quiry about~~ question of ^the weight.
I have no hesitation in ^much saying a ~~twisted~~
line as you made is ^^heavier bulk for
bulk undressed at all events – ~~every thing~~
goes to make it ~~more of~~ more dense – ~~there is~~
^are

Grant's Headed Accounts Sheet, Baron Taylor's Lane (back).

Grant moved to Inverness in 1887 to start up a fishing rod and tackle business in Inverness. This headed accounts sheet (back) is for his premises at 7 Baron Taylor's Lane, at the back of which was a hairdressing shop. Mr. Grant has used the sheet to draft a reply (intended recipient unknown) on the subject of fishing lines.

twisted ~~threads~~ in the first and then the retwisting in making the line &c. I am much interested in this and wd like you to ~~get on with~~ prepare for and then as after this one is inspected ~~send~~ if taper can be made right away ~~as soon as you can~~

Yours in haste

Sandy

Telegrams—"GRANT, RODMAKER."
Works—ROWAN BANK, BALLIFEARY

ALEXANDER * GRANT.
SOLE PATENTEE AND MAKER OF THE VIBRATION ROD.
N.B.—Rods of own make only Repaired.

INVERNESS,
7 BARON TAYLOR'S LANE.

Grant's Headed Accounts Sheet, Baron Taylor's Lane (front).

Col Bennet

My dear Sir'

I have to thank you for your very interesting letter only to hand re-dressing for lines. In the first place I do not care for any mixtures ~~~~~~. I have inwardly tried ~~conventions~~ enclosing most of the substances you refer to ~~& & have to~~ discard all ~~~~~~ except boiled linseed any of the substances you mention added to ~~~~~~ tends to harden ~~~~~~ ~~~~~~ since & you quite understand that any ingredient added to harden wont do, ~~~~~~ therefore use only linseed ~~~~~~ & 6 ~~~~~~ up the part to do needed to be done, do it in this way — get a pint or ½ pint of boiled linseed empty the contents into a 2 or 4 ~~treacle~~ tin ~~~~~~ then dip your line or part thereof ~~~~~~ the two coats or leaving of there

Grant's Headed Accounts Sheet, Ballifeary Post Office (back).

199

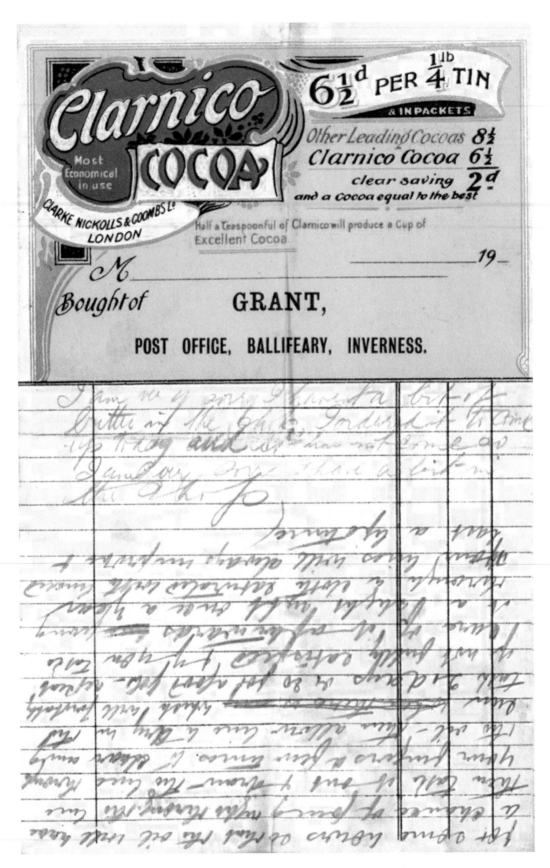

Grant's Headed Accounts Sheet, Ballifeary Post Office (front).

I did not mean that the new line w? be tapered to a finer point than ~~that~~ ~~it~~ that one is as you have it, because as it is it~~s~~ drawn.

~~fine enough for a single Sal Carb & a No 2 or 3 Sal fly - the finer bit can always be added or taken away as desired for Competition or exhibition purposes.

I am very glad you have gone on with the ~~idea~~ idea for the making of a Rall ~~It~~ from your description ~~deal from the beginning~~ however I take it the taper you made can ~~not be~~ not correct - too level or long. I sh? say you w? require to take out a thread every question of half yd. in your ~~weight~~ weight.

I have no hesitation in saying a twisted line as you made us heavier bulk for bulk undressed at all events - everything goes to make it ~~not~~ more dense - ~~are~~ are

twisted ~~friends~~ in the first ^read^ & then
the re twisting in making the line &c.
I am ~~much~~ interested in this &
w⁴ like you to ~~~prepare for~~~ and then
as after this one is inspected, ~~send it~~ the con of
taper can be made ^right^ away
~~as soon as you can~~
Yours in haste

Sandy

Telegrams—"GRANT, RODMAKER."

Works—ROWAN BANK, BALLIFEARY.

7 BARON TAYLOR'S LANE.

ALEXANDER ∗ GRANT,

INVERNESS,

SOLE PATENTEE AND MAKER OF THE VIBRATION ROD.

N.B.—Rods of own make only Repaired.

I

Grant's Headed Accounts Sheet, Baron Taylor's Lane (front).

Items of Correspondence written by Grant:

To be the "Amateur" Fly Casting Champion is a
prized & enviable distinction, and the approach
of another Angling season is a fitting time to learn
such a being's admirable qualities and the superiority of the rods he uses. There are many Anglers
who are interested in any noteworthy achievement
in their art and they would like to have more
proof to thoroughly establish the genuineness
of the different claims which have lately been
heard ~~of~~ about. The recognised Champion at present
is Mr Kerss of Spiriston who fairly won his
title by beating all comers at the tournaments
held on the Thames some years ago, and as he
has not been defeated in competition by
any of the recent claimants I do not see
how their modesty allows them to deprive
so summarily of his laurels without giving
him a chance to retain them

Using the warrantless word "Amateur" does
not confer a patent on any Champion
of being a better caster than one who does
not use it, nor does it protect him
from the obligation of testing his prowess
when challenged though seemingly such
erroneous beliefs do exist. Once upon a time
I regarded any thing in the way of a Champion with
the utmost awe and veneration and was eagerly
anxious to see him put forth his super human
powers in casting and switching. Recently however
I am sorry to say that I have had some experience of
the species. and I am compelled to state
that their confidence in their ability to give

Champion Fly Casters, page 1.

203

This draft letter/article (undated) was written by Grant. It is on the subject of champion fly casters.

the Spectators an "eye-opener" is only matched by their lamentable failure to do any thing of the kind. The way to know a Champion is otherwise. When you see a fisher with from ten to fifteen yards of line out more than he can cast and blundering cracking & moving the grass & bushes on the bank behind him with his line for all he is worth, then you cannot mistake your man: he is a champion, and an amateur one too. There are many Champions who quietly pursue the even tenor of their way quite unknown to fame. And last year I heard of one who makes small potatoes of all the rest. A Mr McKee asked me to look at an 18 feet Greenheart Salmon rod which he had himself made in his leisure moments & its balancing & putting up he states afforded a welcome change from the labours of his ordinary occupation which was that of a Sexton. Mr Mackie highly recommended the rod as it really had a wonderful record. I was assured that a Mr Houston had thrown a fly with it the stupendous distance of sixty-yards. I was so surprised on hearing this statement that I quite forgot to ask the names of the witnesses for purposes of reference. Now I do not know that Mr Houston claims to be the Amateur fly-Casting Champion of the world but no one can doubt in absence of proof to the contrary that he is indeed the real & only amateur Champion by virtue of his great & unapproachable performance. The sexton with the modesty that distinguishes our greatest men stated that he did not cast sixty yds with the rod himself his longest throw being 40 yds with the worm. It might be supposed that Mr Mackie might be overwhelmed with orders for his rods but such was not the case as he did not give them the publicity their merits deserved by means of judicious and laudatory advertisement,

Champion Fly Casters, page 2.

204

Letter to Jock Scott (Donald Rudd) – noted fishing author and friend of Grant

Tomnahurich Farm

Inverness

16th January, 1934

D.S.I. Rudd, Esq.,

"Chalmore"

Manor Way,

Ruslip,

Middlesex.

Dear Sir,

Mr Robb, of Messrs Playfair & Coy., has sent me your letter and manuscript, representing a chapter on "The Planet Cast and Grant Vibration Rod" from another fishing book which you are bringing out. I have carefully read your manuscript and congratulate you on the able manner in which you have elucidated the entire project – the Planet Cast as opposed to artful casting – Rods, with different materials used in their construction – the different balances by different makers, with their varied peculiarities, as against the natural and scientifically made rod. There is little to add or take from your clear and easily defined explanations.

With regard to the paragraph where you write of the constructional features of the rod and its action when in use the ball of <u>each</u> thumb should <u>not</u> lie on the back of the handle. The ball of the upper hand thumb certainly must but the lower hand grip is made similar to a ball socket joint, with the rubber button placed in the palm of the hand. And with the thumb and one or two of the fingers circling easily round upper part of the button and butt-end ferrule. Placing both thumb balls on the back of the handle <u>hinders</u> the application and evenness throughout. Re its power while casting the rod has not only one grip but several, Viz:- In a double-handed rod the upper hand grip is used in the manner of a moveable fulcrum for more or less power to adjust the leverage, balance and manipulation in proportion to the length of line. It is raised as far as practicable without doubling the rod between the hands, then, lowered slightly bit by bit towards the reel, when the whole leverage or power is put into action.

In the pamphlet issued by Playfair & Coy. There is an illustration showing the rod held with both thumbs on the back of the handle which is misleading and this will be rectified in subsequent issue of the pamphlet.

Mr. Robb tells me he sent you copies of letters I wrote to Capt. Edwards and if you find anything useful in these you are at liberty to make any use of them you please.

The splice used in the "Grant Vibration Rod" is the outcome of the principle on which the rod is made. Its point of contact (joining the parts of the rod) runs through its centre, rocking on itself and cannot slip. The knob on the end of the splice is merely to keep the outer coil of the tying thong from slipping over the end. The rings, which I invented, are combined and moveable, adapting themselves to the oscillations of the rod, and sustains the line throughout. What is called the "upright" ring is a barbarous thing, causing a dead load where fixed – against oscillation – never sustaining the line, which bellies out and in between each ring when casting, a state of affairs which in practical fly-casting is simply preposterous. When I see a fly rod with upright rings it prejudices me against the rod, line and wielder.

I think I have said all I have to say now but if you have any further query on which you may think I can assist do not hesitate to write me.

Wishing you every success.

Yours faithfully.

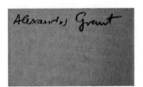

Dear Mr Rudd,

It was with extreme pleasure that I read you triumphant letter with enclosures. It gave me the merriest laugh I have had for a long time. Your Laudatory praise of the 10ft. vibration rod, and the results obtained without any former trials with same, is simply surprising, and it is enhanced by the astonishment of your friend, who, on his first off-go, got ensnared and with some difficulty and expressive languish got himself released from his perplexing position, and who yet on his second attempt succeeded in getting out the very creditable length of 25 yards. Your letter, from beginning to end is very interesting. Your sport in fishing Blagdon Lake for 14 seasons, with an average weight per fish of 3 lbs, 2 ozs. is truly great. As a purely trout loch I know of no other where your average weight per fish can be got. The paper tracing of the 3 ½ Lb brown trout you caught is admirably shaped and the way in which you fish the lake from the side could not be improved upon. Before taking an open shop in the rod and tackle business I made and sold flies wholesale to standard patterns and some to my own liking, dark for dull days and after sunset, but, in all my experience, I have never seen a fly like the one you have sent to me. It is unique, having the whole wing feathers with stems tied with their backs tied to the shoulder of the body. To my mind with each movement of the lift of the rod, the fly becomes stationary, when the feathers rise and take to their natural shape (curve) as if going to fly away, and therein, it seems to me, lies its wonderful merit. More power to you whether the idea of such a fly originated in your own fertile brain or not. Having tried the rod on the golf links I presume you are a golfer and if so, you will have observed that the true golf club swing is similar to the correct method of casting. The throwing of a stone or ball is another good example as you say yourself. Funnily enough, when I used to teach the planet cast, I invariably picked up a stone at the water-side to show the simple method of using the rod, which, in the majority of cases ended in failure, like the golfer who cannot adapt himself to the correct swing of the club.

Your illustrations, giving the different positions when casting, are clearly shown and easily to be understood, both for lifting and driving. You are also right when casting overhead in turning nearly sideways to the line and lifting the rod right across the chest, which enables one to use the power needed for sport or long casting. I thoroughly believe, when you get the length of the Vibration Line required and the correct rings adapting themselves to the balance of the rod, without overloading it, you will not only beat my throw of 37 yards (Planet system) but also beat it in many yards overhead and I hope to live to see, or at least to hear, of your doing 40 yds. or more overhead with a 10 ft rod. But that is not yet and you must bear with patience the delay until these lines and rings are made to satisfaction. Upright rings would not only take away power but would not sustain a vibration line from reel to point of rod and, nearing the return of the cast, the part of the line running through these d-----d things would slacken back at the moment the drive forward is made, giving an uneven result unequal to the power used. Here again comes in the sustained swing of a golf club or the throw of a stone from a firm foundation to show the fallacy of using such defective impediments in fly fishing.

Now for other matters. It is quite possible the Loch Ness "monster" went up the River Ness when in spate as, with the locks, it could not reach the loch via the Canal. Tomnahurich is not purely a Gaelic word. Tomna of course in Gaelic means Hill of and the commonly accepted meaning of the word Hill of Fairies but Gaelic speaking people hereabouts give the translation as Hill of the Yew tree. It could also mean Hill of the harlots. The hill itself is perhaps one of the most unique cemeteries in the world and is in shape like an upturned boat. My present farm is adjacent to it. If you can come north this length in the summer I shall be more than delighted to see you and we can then have a talk about rods, fishing, etc. and perhaps casting trials from the banks of the river Ness near the place where I hooked and landed a salmon 47 yards out. Since disposing of the rights of manufacture of the Vibration rod I have pursued my own theories on the law of gravitation and nature with the result that nearly 20 years ago I discovered (what I could not find in the Euclidean third dimension) a fourth dimension – Relativity but to explain this would require a new vocabulary. Briefly, I find that the measurements of the 3rd dimensional spacing will not agree anywhere with acoustical spacing. The 4th does. In dealing with the vibrations in a material the relationship of the acoustics of the different parts supercedes all else. This may possibly sound like Greek to you but at this theory I am now working, and working against time too as I am now aged 73. I am trying to complete the key to the foregoing (which is a stringed instrument absolutely true, with resonance like to the human voice) and when finished the principle can be applied universally. Anything from the smallest vibration article to the most complex can be made complete in itself and no chance work. Though in a thousand pieces the parts can be related one to the other, all laid aside separately, and when put together – a <u>oneness</u> - - with no overtones or overbalance.

More of this when I shall have the pleasure of seeing you. I shall keep the photo of Blagdon Lake and also the paper tracing of your 5 lb brown trout.

The old Spanish greeting with which you conclude your most interesting letter is new to me and I heartily reciprocate the kindly wish contained therein.

With kind regards,

Yours sincerely,

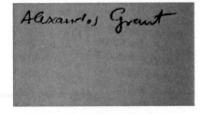

The Inverness Courier Friday 1 – 1 – 1937:

A FAMOUS INVERNESS ANGLER

The World's Champion Fly Caster

It is interesting to note that Mr Alexander Grant, the leader of the Highland Strathspey and Reel Society, who was honoured on Wednesday evening, has a very high reputation as an angler. He was well known to former generations of anglers, and his prowess with the rod on river and loch was known not only locally but throughout Scotland and England. He has the distinction of being the inventor and maker of the "Grant Vibration Rod", and has other achievements at his credit as an angler, being at one time the Champion British caster. His great personal friend, "Jock Scott", the famous angling writer, has in many of his books much to say about Mr Grant. We have taken the liberty of quoting what "Jock Scott" wrote in his well-known book, "Game Fish Records" about Mr Grant who has an autographed copy in his possession. The fly-leaf bears the following: -"To Battan, World's record salmon fly caster, from 'Jock Scott'. With best wishes and thanks – October 1936". The extract is as follows:-

MR ALEXANDER GRANT.

In all probability the modern reader has forgotten, or never heard of, the salmon-fly casting controversy of the "nineties", in which Mr Grant took a principal part; but no book of records would be complete without a list of his achievements. He was of course, the inventor of the famous Vibration rod, and caused very considerable argument, culminating in a regular newspaper "war".

If any of my readers have access to back numbers of the "Fishing Gazette" and "Land and Water" covering the years 1895- 97 they will see with what vigour – almost ferocity – the dispute was carried on! In these days we argue in a more "refaned" manner. Perhaps the law has been tightened up – some of those old letters sounded distinctly libellous!

Mr Grant, the fons et origo of the whole trouble, fished the Ness, the Freeday water, open to residents in the burgh every eight day was his principal fishing ground. This stretch is very wide, and, naturally, soundly flogged, so the Ness angler became of necessity a long distance caster, or caught no fish. Mr Grant spent many hours trying to improve his rod and so outcast his fellows, but, becoming disgusted at his lack of success gave up fishing until he could make a rod capable of out casting any yet known. He was a musician and when experimenting with fiddles, discovered the principle of vibration frequencies. This he applied to fly rod. Very briefly, the idea is this: the density of wood varies – being a natural product – hence two rods made to similar dimensions, length and diameter, will have varying actions, due to the different density of the wood from which they are made. The pieces of rod likewise differ for the same reason. Mr Grant discovered that by "tuning" each part of the rod to the same vibration-frequency, or not, a perfect action and balance was secured. This, in conjunction with his patent splice, produced an extremely powerful rod, since each part was springing in entire unity with the rest, and being adjusted to the same frequency, no part was quicker or slower than the others, thus marring the action.

An eye-witness has given me an account of the rod's debut on the river Ness. Suffice it to say that Mr Grant outcast all his fellow-anglers by ten yards, and, covering fish they could not reach, landed several salmon. Immediately he became famous, and likewise a specialist in hooking salmon at hitherto un-heard of distances. To this day, in Inverness, they will point out the spot where Mr Grant hooked one of the farthest-off fish.

At that time certain anglers made a hobby of looking for taking fish in far-out lies and bringing word to Mr Grant so that he could try for them. Of these, the late Mr Watson, of Inverness, was one. One day, a day of high water, Mr Watson marked a taking fish at the "General's Well" and informed Mr Grant. Upon arrival at the water they found a few fishers and a large body of spectators (Inverness, as a whole, is very keen on fishing). The fish was lying in the backwater at the offside of the bridge, and, in spite of trying from various anglers, none of the assembled anglers could reach the fish with a fly. (For the benefit of those who know the Ness, the bridge mentioned is the footbridge to the islands; about 150 yards above this bridge the river divides, causing islands). The fish was still rising when Mr Grant arrived. He was using heavy line, strong cast and a 2-inch 4/0 double iron. Obviously, such heavy gear required casting downstream at an acute angle in order to avoid bellying the line. The spectators burst into advice:- "No use casting from there; you'll never reach him!". Mr Grant, however, commenced to cast and, gradually getting out line, hooked and killed a salmon of 8 lb. The distance from Mr Grant's stance to the backwater was afterwards measured and proved to be 47 yards! All things considered, this must be regarded as one of the most notable fly-fishing feats on record, especially as, owing to a high bank, Mr Grant was switching.

An interesting fact in connection with Mr Grant's long-distance fishing is that he never tried to strike a salmon when using a very long line. I have been told that he invariably hooked his fish on these occasions very firmly, provided, of course, that the fly was swimming correctly. Probably this was due to the fact that a fly, when fished on a very long line, comes over the fish much slower than one attached to a very short line. Mr Grant is reported to have said – "The surest-hooked fish, all else being equal, is with a long line and none of this.....nonsense about "hitting a fish on the rise!"".

Mr Grant afterwards cast from an anchored boat on the Ness, when he cast the amazing distance of 65 yards with a 21 –foot rod and 61 yards with an 18-foot rod. The judge was the late Mr J. H. Corballis, J.P., of Inverness and Moniack Castle, author of "Forty-five Years Sport". The runner-up in this competition cast the astonishing length of 56 yards with a 21-foot rod. What a spectacle.

Then Mr Grant journeyed south, and in 1896 gave his celebrated exhibition in Kinston-on-Thames. Such well known judges as the late Mr R. B. Marston, Mr Crawshay and Mr Wilson of "Rod and Gun" and the angling editors of "Land and Water" and "The Field" attended: and all measurements were made from the caster's foot to the point where the fly hit the water – the casts being made parallel to the bank. At that time the record cast was an "overhead", with line shot, of 49 yards 1 foot, to the credit of the late John Enright of Castle Conel. To everyone's surprise, Mr Grant used the "Planet" cast – a pure switch – and shot no line. His figures, when published created a veritable furore. Here they are (from the "Fishing Gazette"):-

Mr Grant cast on three separate afternoons.

Thursday, December 10, Mr Grant, steady breeze downstream, 15 inches above water level: 20 – foot rod, 56 yards; 18 foot 5 – inch rod, 54 yards; 10 foot rod, 37 yards.

Friday, December 11, Mr Grant, 19 – foot rod, 53 yards 5 inches; 16 – foot 10 inch rod, 49 yards 1 foot.

Saturday, December 12, Mr Grant, 20 – foot rod, 54 yards 2 foot 6 inches; 18 – foot 5 inch rod, 53 yards 1 foot.

These records were the subject of much ink slinging, which eventually developed into a discussion of casting methods. The two chief camps were composed of those who favoured natural conditions, i.e. the holding of tournaments on salmon rivers where obstacles existed and Spey and switch casting was needed as well as overhead; and those who maintained that overhead casting from a boat or stage was the right and proper method. The former were anxious to ban any shooting of line, maintaining, with a certain show of reason, that the true test of rod and man was the amount of line that could be picked off the water.

The "war" of course, eventually died down and nothing definite was done. This, I think, was unfortunate, for a grand opportunity existed to prove, once and for all, the best all-round salmon rod and the champion angler. The would-be competitors, however, were unable to agree as to the conditions. As originally suggested, the idea was to pit one man and one rod only against the tape, i.e. each competitor was to use the same rod to execute the overhead, the Spey, the switch and the underhand. The competitor who put up the longest distance in each and every cast was to be declared champion. Nowadays the competitor is at liberty to use a special rod for each type of cast, hence the salmon rod continues in many cases to be a special instrument for carrying out one particular type of cast.

To return to Mr Grant. He belonged to the select company of anglers who have landed a 50 lb salmon, his largest fish being a 55-pounder caught at the river Garry in September 1887 at the outlet from Loch Quoich. The fish was caught in a Thunder and Lightening fly.

Another record which he claimed was that of casting 74 yards overhead upon the grass. This was done at Kingston-on-Thames during his previously mentioned casting exhibition, and was duly measured by the judges. It was undertaken solely to prove his contention that a rod which could lift 50 yards of line on water could lift a further 20 yards on grass. The line was laid out on the grass then cast overhead. To my mind, one of the amazing features in connection with Mr Grant's exploits is his small physique. It was a very different matter, when Mr John Enright appeared on the riverside; a strongly-built, burly man, he looked the part, yet his record of 49 yards 1 foot was beaten. Mr Grant was asked at Kingston to what he attributed his great manual dexterity in handling a fly rod. He is reported to have answered – "When I was a youngster I went in for forestry; swinging a seven-pound axe is the finest training you can have". Will future expert casters emulate Mr Grant and the great Mr Gladstone and proceed to chop down trees? I wonder if it is really necessary? If so, then casting schools must be equipped with forests and axes! (Principals of casting schools please note!).

I have seen an interesting letter written by Mr Grant concerning the Ness. He says, speaking of the Free day water:- "I can imaging a practical fisher viewing the scene on a free day; seven or eight fishers in line one after the other slashing the water; he would naturally expect only one or at most the two in front to catch fish, which generally was the case, because the salmon got scared and moved further out. It is slightly different if fresh fish are running into the pools, which some of the more experienced fishers depended on. It needs a very long and very good caster to reach the scared fish, whipped outside the bounds of an ordinary angler's cast. The Ness needs an absolutely accurately-thrown line cast at the angle to suit the stream, so that the fly shall swim as soon as it lands in the water, line taught from the reel, and no splash. Then, if you refrain from trying to hit the rising fish, you will get them". To the best of my knowledge that prescription holds good to-day, and I will add that the Ness angler is as good a caster as you will find anywhere – watch him switching!

The cast which Mr Grant invented, the Planet, is in great favour in Inverness. It possess many advantages; the line is not snatched off the water as in the overhead, but gently lifted; a line lying parallel to the bank can be picked up and projected across the stream with ease; it requires less effort than the Spey and the fly has not to be accurately dropped by the angler's toe; it is easiest to learn, can be used on running or still water, and requires very little effort. Personally, I wish it were more widely known – on the Ness it is a sine qua non, since obstacles on the bank are no hinderance to its execution.

Mr Grant's name will live; as one of the great casters of his day he is a notable figure in the salmon-angling world.

Alexander 'Battan' Grant

1856 - 1942

(Fisherman, Musician & Fiddler of Note)

Part 4

The Master Violin Makers

Tonal and Vibrational Properties of Violins - and the Physics of Harmonic Wood.

The Violin

Man's greatest challenge to replicate the human voice with a bowed stringed instrument.

It would be something of a truism to say that Grant was fairly consumed by his desire to improve on the tonal qualities of the violins which he built. Hours and hours of dedicated effort must have gone into making and improving the tonal vibrational qualities of his violins. So much so, as presented earlier and in Figure 1, he developed his own concept for the body of the instrument which he called a 'Rondello'. Grant made around six of these, including work on a 'Roncello' - the sound box of one of these is held in the IMAG store room.

Figure 1 A Grant Rondello on Display at IMAG

He did not succeed in his efforts, but it could be said that he did not fail in making a type of instrument which has decided physical similarities to other bowed stringed instruments, such as the Chinese Huqin, Figure 2, of which there are a multitude of variants (roughly around 80 have been catagorised). These instruments have been around for much longer periods in history than Grant's, possibly even more so than the violin – so where did Grant get his idea from, or was it completely out of his own head?

Inverness always had its own harbour. Perhaps a sailor or shipping trader could have had the first type of disc-shaped violin or single-stringed instrument with something akin to a tin can or box shape at the bottom to amplyfy the sound. Had he seen one of these instruments before is a question which we cannot answer. [Was there a Chinese fore-runner to 'Sunny Jim' in Neil Munroe's classic 'The Vital Spark', siting on deck of an evening plonking away?]

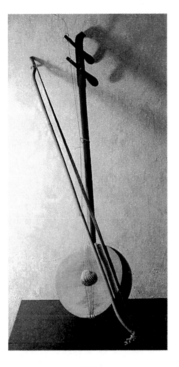

Figure 2 A Chinese Huqin

This, of course, is speculation, but surprisingly there is a great deal of speculation even in the modern world when it comes to analysing the tonal qualities of a violin, and why the great Cremonese masters of the craft could make such good instruments. It can be said without any speculation that Grant failed in his pursuit of perfection for a number of reasons, not least because the construction of a disc-shaped fiddle with seven internal sound posts was going to be very difficult to achieve, coupled with a lack of adequate sound projection. He had no recourse to scientific instruments which could aid his analysis of the harmonics of the instument, no heritage to fall back on in the making of violins which the great masters of the craft had built up over hundreds of years.

He did, however, succeed in making very good playable violins, if the opinions of the top fiddlers in the Highlands are anything to go by. Those who have played on the Grant violin in Morisons Ironmongers in Beauly have praised the tonal qualities of the instrument.

What Makes a Great Violin?

The violin is the most highly developed and most sophisticated of all stringed instruments. It emerged in Northern Italy about 1550, in a form that has remained essentially unchanged ever since. The famous Cremonese violin-making families of Amati, Stradivari and Guarneri formed a continuous line of succession that flourished from about 1600 to 1750, with skills being handed down from father to son and from master to apprentice.

Violins by the great Italian makers are, of course, beautiful works of art in their own right, and are coveted by collectors as well as players. Particularly outstanding ones have reputedly changed hands for over a million pounds. In contrast, fine modern instruments typically cost about £10,000, while factory-made violins for beginners can be bought for under £100. Do such prices really reflect such large differences in quality?

The Myths and Unknowns

Anecdote: During the course of producing this book, two or three violins with a Stradivarius label inside came up for auction at the Dingwall Auction Mart. As is well known, cows and sheep are the usual trading items, so an alert purchaser will most likely realise that this is a most unlikely place to find a Stradivarius violin at a cheap price.

When enquiring of a violin up for auction, the sale room assistant jokingly (I thought!) said it would be a Stradivari – he proceeded to his office and returned holding a magnifying glass. Low and behold there was the famous name printed in presumably authentic manner visible inside, on what looked like a label that had been stained with tea!

Never rely on the label inside the violin to spot a fake instrument as the label will probably have been forged as well.

It is interesting to note however, that Grant worked on (and 'improved') an instrument which he believed to be a Stradivari. This instrument is held at IMAG, awaiting the inspection of any historian of violins, see Part 1. However, the carving of the f-holes often helps to identify the maker of a valuable instrument.

Wood

Stradivarius violins are famous for their beautiful tone, and for years musicians, violin makers and scientists have wondered what makes these instruments so special. One theory is that it is at least in part due to the spruce wood used. The best violins are made from very hard, dense wood produced by slow-growing trees. By looking at the growth rings in the wood, scientists have found that, although the density of the wood used in modern and old violins is relatively similar, there is a big difference when comparing the early and late growth rings. The legendary Stradivarius violins have a much lower density difference than modern versions, which affects the vibrational efficiency and thus sound production. Scientists believe the unique density is due to the 'Little Ice Age' that hit Europe from the mid-1400s to the mid1800s, which meant cooler summers and longer winters. The trees that Antonio Stradivari used to make his violins between 1680 and 1720 would therefore have been even more slow growing than normal throughout their lifetime.

The wood – spruce for the top, willow for the internal blocks and linings, and maple for the back, ribs, and neck – grew during the Maunder Minimum, characterised by harsh winters and short summers that led to slower growth and more uniform annual rings. It is important to know that the speed of sound in wood increases with stiffness – the resistance of an elastic body to deformation by an applied force – of the material, and decreases with the density. All wood decay fungi reduce density, but the majority also reduce the speed of sound.

The Scientific Challenge

Modern science has now found that the application of the vegetative state of two fungi, Physisporinus vitreous for the top plate, and Xylaria for the bottom plate, which have thread-like cells will actively colonise the wood. These fungi secrete enzymes which can ultimately alter the wood structure and its acoustic properties. Once an optimum wood density loss has been induced in the top and bottom plates by the wood decay fungi, the wood can be sterilised with ethylene oxide, killing the bacteria and fungi. An important side effect of the fungal treatment is the reduction of the often irritating high notes of a violin, and makes the instrument sound warmer and mellower.

The consequence of this process is that wood density is reduced; damping is increased, while the modulus of elasticity remains unchanged. The method can improve the acoustic properties of resonance wood – particularly as it is becoming increasingly difficult to find superior resonance wood due to the impact of global warming.

Did Stradivarius have a secret?

Many theories have been put forward to claim that Stradivarius did have a secret method which he used in the construction of his violins. The most popular for well over a century has been that the varnish had some sort of 'magic' composition. The main function of the varnish is to protect the instrument from dirt and to stop it absorbing moisture from the players hands. This also imparts great aesthetic value to the instrument, with its translucent coating highlighting the beautiful grain structure of the wood below.

However, historical research has shown that the varnish is no different to that used by many furniture makers when Stradivari was alive. Researchers at Cambridge University, for example, have used electron microscopy to identify many of the important ingredients of the varnish itself, and the materials that are used to smooth the surface before the varnish is applied. It turns out that most could easily have been bought from the pharmacist shop next to Stradivari's workshop. Apart from the possibility that the varnish was contaminated with the wings of passing insects and debris from the workshop floor, there is no convincing evidence to support the idea of a secret formula!

Indeed, ultraviolet photography has revealed that many fine-sounding Italian violins have lost almost all their original varnish, and were recoated during the 19th century or later. The composition of the varnish is therefore unlikely to be the long-lost secret, although too much varnish would certainly increase the damping and therefore sully the tone.

Other researchers, meanwhile, have claimed that Stradivari's secret was to soak the wood in water, to leach out supposedly harmful chemicals, before it was seasoned. Although this would be consistent with the idea that the masts and oars of recently sunken Venetian war galleys might have been used to make violins, the scientific and historical evidence to support this view is unconvincing.

This raises the first point of contention – is there really a lost secret that sets Stradivarious violins apart from the best instruments made in Grant's time or indeed today? After more than a hundred years of vigorous debate, this question remains highly contentious, provoking strongly held but divergent views among playes, violin makers and scientists alike. All of the greatest violinists of modern times certainly believe it to be true, and invariably perform on violins by Stradivari or Guarneri in preference to modern instruments. The popular belief is that their unsurpassed skills, together with the magical 'Stradivarius secret', were lost by the start of the 19th century.

The choice of high-quality wood for making instruments has always been recognized by violin makers, and well-seasoned wood is generally recommended. However, by measuring the pattern of growth-rings in the wood of a Stradivarius, it is revealed that the Italian violin makers sometimes used planks of wood that had only been seasoned for five years. However, such wood is now 300 years old, and the intrinsic internal damping will almost certainly have decreased with time, as the internal organic structure has dried out.

The same will obviously be true for all old Italian instruments. The age of the wood may therefor automatically contribute to the improved quality of the older instruments. This may also explain why the quality of a modern instrument appears to change in its first few years. Surprisingly, many players still believe that their instruments improve because they are loved and played well, which would be very difficult to explain on any rational scientific basis!

Over the last 150 years, physicists have made considerable progress in understanding the way the violin works. In the 19th century the 'modernized' Stradivarius violin emerged with an 'enhanced' tone as a result of scientifically guided 'improvements' by the leading violin restorers of the day. However, Stradivari would be amazed to find that the modern musical world credits him with such a secret. After all, how could he possibly have had the clairvoyance to foresee that his instruments would be extensively modified in the 19th century to produce the kind of sound we value so highly today? Indeed, those sounds would have been totally alien to the musical tastes of his time.

Science has not provided any convincing evidence for the existence or otherwise of any measurable property that would set the Cremonese instruments apart from the finest violins made by skilled craftsmen today. Indeed, some leading soloists do occasionally play on modern instruments. However, the really top soloists, and, not surprisingly, violin dealers, who have a vested interest in maintaining the Cremonese legend of intrinsic superiority, remain unconvinced.

Quality and Excellence of Craftmanship

Every violin, whether a Stradivarius or the cheapest factory made copy, has a distinctive 'voice' of its own. Just as any musician can immediately recognise the difference between the voices of great Opera singers singing the same operatic aria, so a skilled violinist can distinguish between different qualities in the sound produced by individual Stradivari or Guarneri violins. The ability to do so represents a high challenge to express in scientific terms and to quantify (in numbers) how this is achieved. The challenge from a scientific point of view is to characterise such differences by physical measurements. Indeed, over the last century and a half, many famous physicists have been intrigued by the workings of the violin, with Helmholtz, Savart and Raman all making vital contributions.

However, it is important to recognize that the sound of the great Italian instruments we hear today is very different from the sound they would have made in Stradivari's time. Almost all Cremonese instruments underwent extensive restoration, and "improvement" in the 19th century. You need only listen to 'authentic' baroque groups, in which most top performers play on fine Italian instruments restored to their former state, to recognize the vast difference in tone quality between these restored originals and 'modern' versions of the Cremonese violins.

Prominent among the 19th century violin restorers was the French maker Vuillaume. Vuillaume worked closely with Felix Savart, best known to physicists for the Biot-Savart law in electromagnetism, to enhance the tone of early instruments. Vuillaume, Savart and others wanted to produce more powerful and brilliant sounding instruments that could stand out in the larger orchestras and concert halls of the day. Improvements in instrument design were also introduced to support the technical demands of great violin virtuosi such as Paganini.

Naturally - The Importance of Build Quality

So how do skilled violin makers optimize the tone of an instrument during the construction process? They begin by selecting a wood of the highest possible quality for the front and back plates, which they test by tapping with a hammer and judging how well it rings.

The next important step is to skilfully carve the plates out of the solid wood, taking great care to obtain the right degree of arching and variations in thickness. The craftsman has to learn how to adjust the plates to produce a fine-sounding instrument. Traditional makers optimise the thickness by testing the 'feel' of the plates when they are flexed, and by the sounds produced when they are tapped at different positions with the knuckles. This is the traditional equivalent of nodal analysis, with the violin maker's brain providing the interpretative computing power.

However, in the last 50 years or so, a group of violin makers has emerged who have tried to take a more overtly scientific approach to violin making. The pioneer in this field was Carleen Hutchins, the doyenne of violin acoustics in the US. She founded the Catgut Society of America in 1958, together with William Saunders of 'Russel-Saunders coupling' fame and John Schelling, a former director of radio research at Bell Labs. The society brings together violin makers and scientists from across the world, with the common aim of advancing our understanding of violin acoustics and developing scientific methods to help makers improve the quality of their instruments.

One common practice that has been adopted by violin makers has been to replace the traditional flexing and tapping of plates by controlled measurements. During the carving process, the thinned plates are suspended horizontally above a large loudspeaker. The acoustic resonances excited by it can readily be identified by sprinkling glitter onto the surface of the plates. When the loudspeaker has excited a resonance, the glitter bounces up and down, and moves towards the nodal lines of the resonant modes excited, much as in the same way that iron fillings, when placed above a bar magnet on a sheet of paper, will display the field lines of the magnet when tapped. The aim is to interactively thin or 'tune' the first few free-plate resonances to specified frequencies and nodal patterns.

Unfortunately, there are very few examples of such measurements for really fine Italian instruments because their owners are naturally reluctant to allow them to be taken apart for the sake of science. The relatively few tests that have been performed suggest that the early Italian makers may have tuned the resonant modes of the individual plates – which they could identify as they tapped them – to exact musical intervals. This would be consistent with the prevailing Renaissance view of 'perfection', which was measured in terms of numbers and exact ratios.

Members of the 'scientific' school of violin makers might reasonably claim that this could be the lost Stradivarius secret. However, it must indeed have been a secret, since there is no historical evidence to support the case. Although many first-class modern violins have been built based on these principles, there is little evidence to suggest that they are any better than many fine instruments made with more traditional methods.

However, neither traditional craftmanship nor scientific methods can hope to control the detailed resonant structure of an instrument in the acoustically important range above 1 kHz. Even the tiniest changes in the thickness of the plates will significantly affect the specific resonances in this frequency range. Furthermore, the frequencies and distribution of the resonant modes of the violin depend on the exact position of the sound post, which imposes an additional constraint on the modes that can be excited. Top players regularly return their instruments to violin makers, who move the sound post and adjust the bridge in an effort to optimize the sound. This means that there is no unique set of vibrational characteristics for any particular instrument – not even a Stradivarius!

As noted above, a key factor that affects the quality of a violin is the internal damping of the wood. This strongly affects the multi-resonant response of the instrument and the overall background at high frequencies. In particular, the difference between the peaks and troughs of the resonant response is determined by the quality-factor of the resonances. This largely depends on internal losses within the wood when it vibrates: only a small fraction of the energy is lost by acoustic radiation.

How Did the Great Masters Produce the Instruments Shape?

It goes without saying that the violin is a unique instrument in more ways than one – particularly with reference to its outline shape. How was it that the great masters came to design their instruments in such a uniform way with so little variation on the dimensions between makers? Over the centuries the shape has converged to what we are all familiar with today. The following method is described by Kerr based on work by Morgan and Reid.

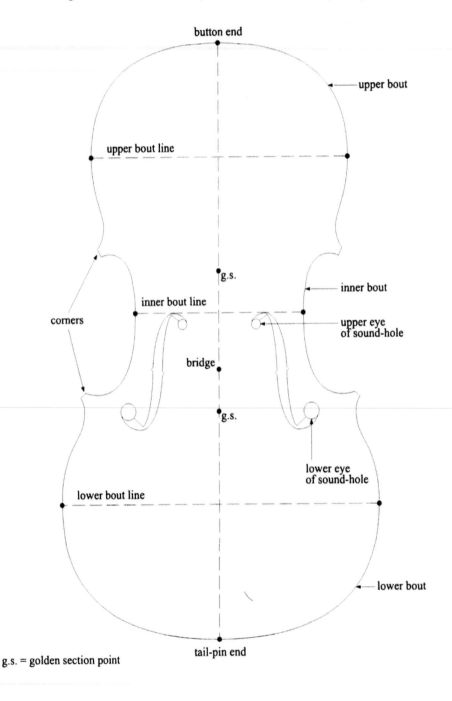

Figure 3 Principle Defining Features of a Violin

Surprisingly as it may seem, it appears that they were using the same rule as the master painters who preceded them used to create the division of geometric space on their canvas. Using modern equipment, these construction lines can now be made visible beneath the paint on some Leonardo works and several others. The technique was not a secret as such and would have been known by the Cremonese violin makers. This rule is termed the 'Golden Rule', in which the whole is equal to the sum of the lesser plus the greater part. A golden section can be created from a single dimension, e.g. say in this case the length you wish to make the body of the violin (AB). Locating C at its mid-point extend a line to cut a normal (90 degree) line AD. From C, CD describes an arc to intersect BA extended at E. A is the golden section point and divides BE in the golden ratio. The rule holds for any dimension and is always equal to 1.618…….181818 on and on. This is shown below.

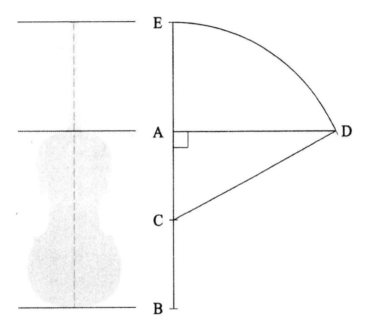

Figure 4 A Golden Ratio Constructed Using a Set of Dividers and a Straight Edge

Intriguingly even the fret spacing on a guitar uses the same method to position them on the finger board, as shown in Figure 5 below, where each successive interspace is 1.618 greater than the previous one. (the Golden ratio is in fact an irrational non-repeating number like pie).

Figure 5 Guitar Frets Spaced in Accordance with the Golden Rule

Hence it transpires that the great master violin makers did not need to resort to any clever mathematics to construct a plan shape for their instruments. They simply used straight lines and ratios of numbers to divide up the space and produce the outline of the instrument. This was quite an astonishing achievement done by using only a starting dimension, with no other numbers added, they could arrive at the defining shape we are all so familiar with as shown in Figures 3, 20 and 21, The method is explained diagrammatically as follows.

Firstly, it is a straight forward task to construct a curved line between any two points using a straight edge as shown below.

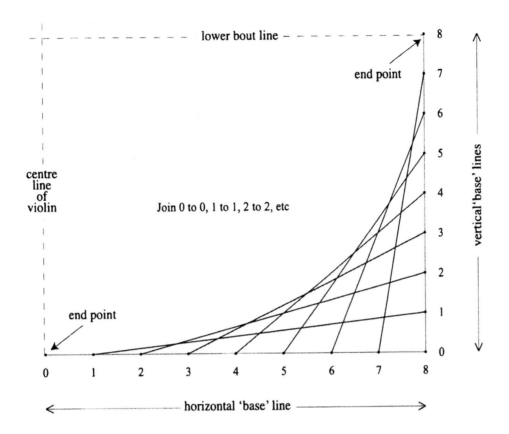

Figure 6 Generating a Curve from Straight Lines

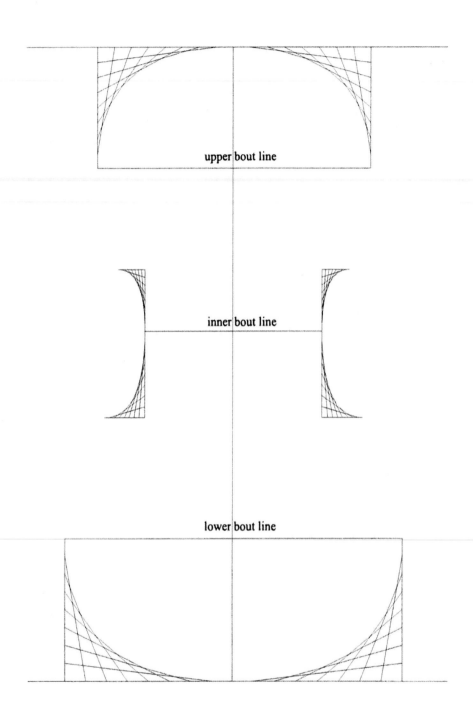

Figure 7 Curved Corners Created by the Method Shown Above

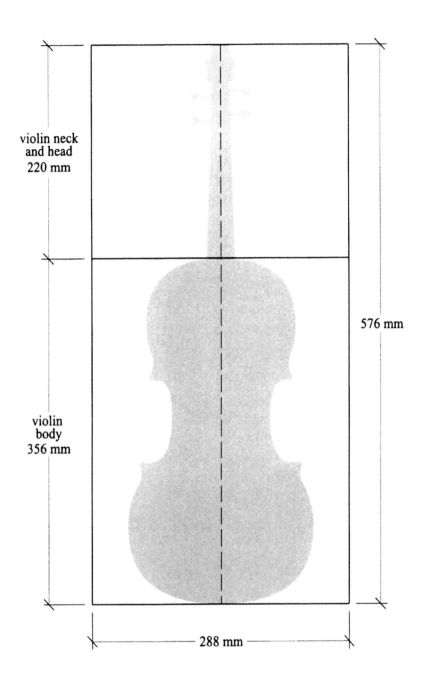

Figure 8 Violin Frame Based on a 2:1 Rectangle

(356 mm, the chosen body length, is within a few mm of the body dimension of a Cremonese violin)

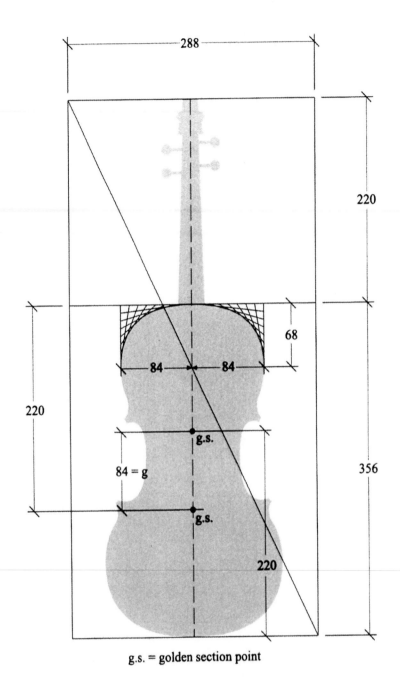

g.s. = golden section point

Figure 9 Straight Edge and Dividers Used to Position the Bouts

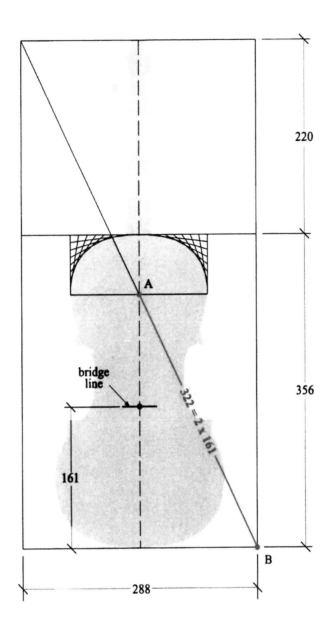

Figure 10 Derivation of the Bridge Line

231

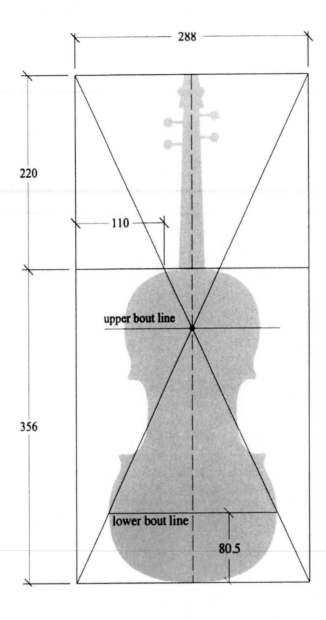

Figure 11 Position and Width of the Lower Bout

from the 2:1 Rectangle

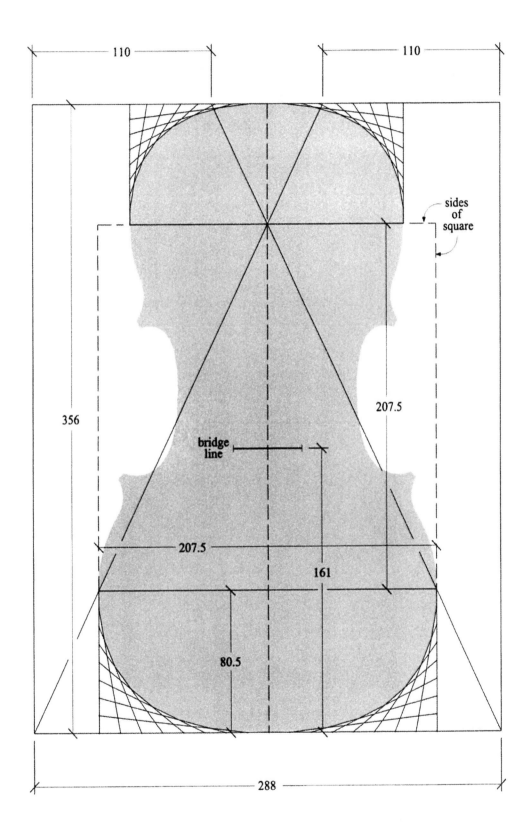

Figure 12 Position and width of the Lower Bout based simply on ratios

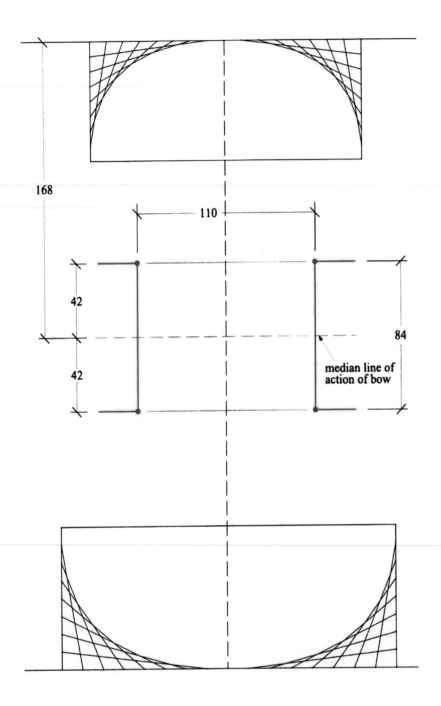

168

110

42

42

84

median line of
action of bow

Figure 13 Locating the Inner Bouts

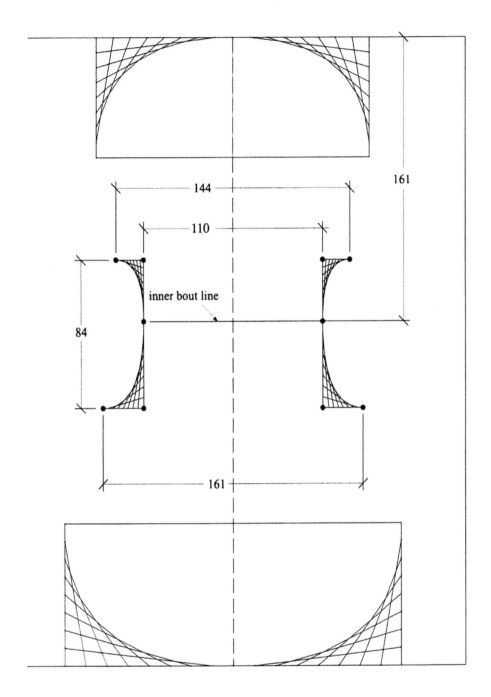

144

110

161

inner bout line

84

161

Figure 14 Generating the Curves of the Inner Bouts

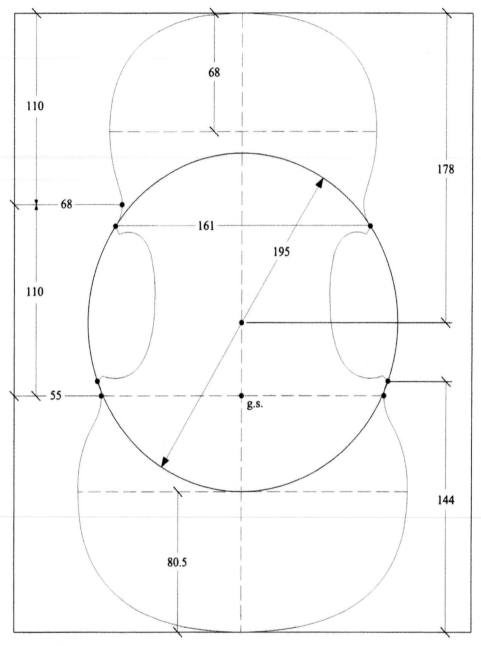

g.s. = golden section point

Figure 15 Locating the Corners

236

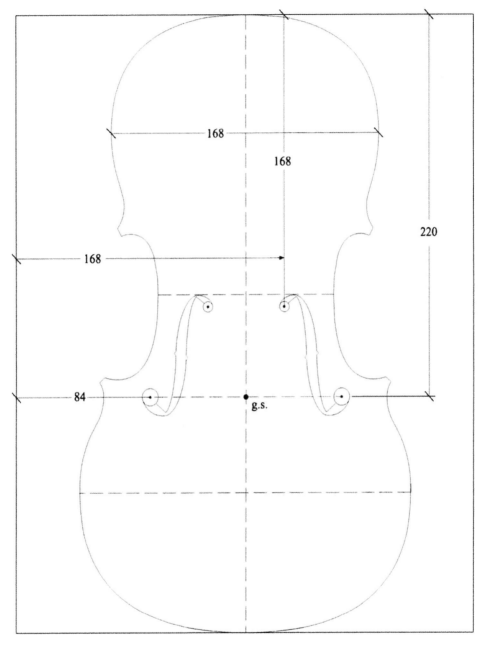

g.s. = golden section point

Figure 16 Locating the Eyes of the Sound Holes

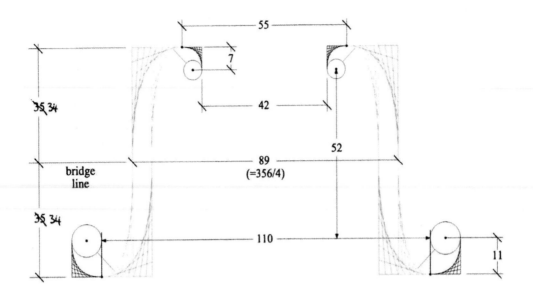

Figure 17 Curves of the Sound Holes

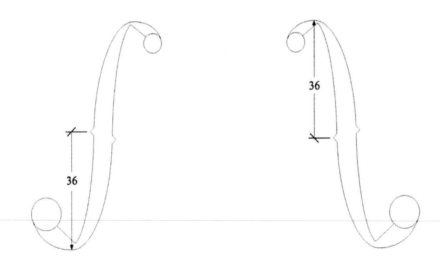

Figure 18 Locating the 'Nicks'

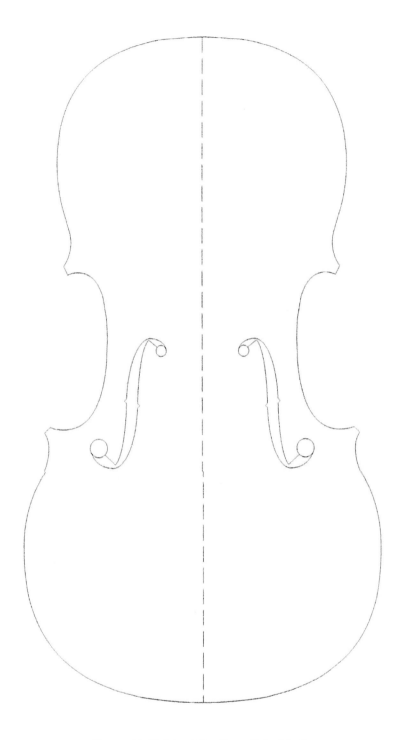

Figure 19 Finished Outline of the Violin

Figure 20 Comparison with the "Betts" Stradivari

Figure 21 Comparison with the "Alard" Stradivari

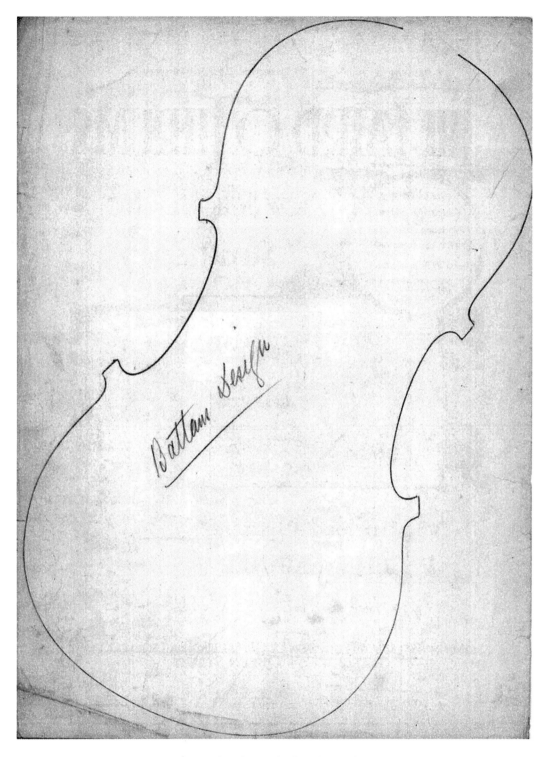

Figure 22 Design for violin by Alexander Grant.

This pencil outline of a fiddle body, named 'Battan Design', is drawn on the reverse of a piece of sheet music in the Grant collection. Grant would most definitely not have used the method just described. How close it resembles any of the instruments he made is a task still to be undertaken - if possible.

The Function of the Main Components of a Violin

The bridge piece and front and back plates are illustrated in Figure 23. Sound is produced by drawing a bow across one or more of the four stretched strings. The string tensions are adjusted by turning pegs at one end of the string, so that their fundamental frequencies are about 200, 300, 440 and 660 Hz – which corresponds to the notes G, D, A and E. However, the strings themselves produces almost no sound.

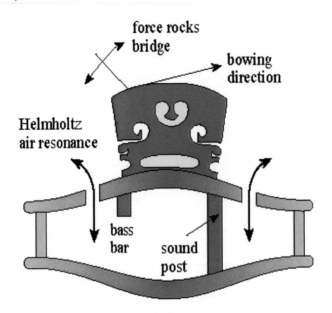

Figure 23 Essential parts of the violin

To produce sound, energy from the vibrating string is transferred to the main body of the instrument – the so-called sound box. The main plates of the violin act rather like a loudspeaker cone, and it is the vibration of these plates that produce most of the sound.

The strings are supported by the 'bridge', which defines the effective vibrating length of the string, and also acts as a mechanical transformer. The bridge converts the transverse forces of the strings into the vibrational modes of the sound box. Because the it has its own resonant modes, it plays a key role in the overall tone of the instrument. It is not entirely clear if Grant made his own bridge pieces as he preferred to buy in some parts - though the illustration shown in Figure 24, from the contents of his work shop, would indicate that he may have made his own.

The front plate is carved from a solid block of fine-grained pine. Maple is usually used for the back plate and pine for the sides. Two expertly carved and elegantly shaped 'f-holes' are also cut into the front plate as shown in Figure 25.

The f-holes play a number of important acoustic roles. By breaking up the area of the front plate, they affect its vibrational modes at the highest frequencies. More importantly, they boost the sound output at low frequencies. This occurs through the 'Helmholtz air resonance', in which air bounces backwards and forwards through the f-holes. The resonant frequency is determined by the area of the f-holes and the volume of the instrument. It is the only acoustic resonance of the instrument over which violin makers have almost complete control.

Figure 24 Bridge pieces held in the Grant collection

Early in the 16th century it was discovered that the output of stringed instruments could be increased by wedging a solid rod – the 'sound post' – between the back and front plates, close to the feet of the bridge. The force exerted by the bowed strings causes the bridge to rock about this position, causing the other side of the plate to vibrate with a larger amplitude. This increases the radiating volume of the violin and produces a much stronger sound.

The violin also has a 'bass bar' glued underneath the top plate, which stops energy being dissipated into acoustically inefficient higher-order modes. The bass bar and sound post were both made bigger in the 19th century to strengthen the instrument and to increase the sound output.

Figure 25 From the Grant collection

The Scientific Analysis of How Strings Vibrate

In the 19th century the German physicist Hermon von Helmholtz showed that when a violin string is bowed, it vibrates in a way that is completely different from the sinusoidal standing waves that are familiar to all physicists. Although the string vibrates back and forth parallel to the bowing direction, Helmholtz showed that other transverse vibrations of the string could also be excited, made up of straight-line sections. These are separated by 'kinks' that travel back and forth along the string and are reflected at the ends. The kinks move with the normal transverse-wave velocity, $c = (T/m)^{1/2}$, where T is the tension and m the mass per unit length of the string. The bowing action excites a Helmholtz mode with a single kink separating two straight sections, Figure 26.

When the kink is between the bow and the fingered end of the string, the string moves at the same speed and in the same direction as the bow. Only a small force is needed to lock the two modes together. This is known as the 'sticking regime' (Figure 26a). But as soon as the kink moves past the bow, on its way to the bridge and back, the string slips past the bow and starts moving in the opposite direction to it. This is known as the 'slipping' regime' (Figure 26b).

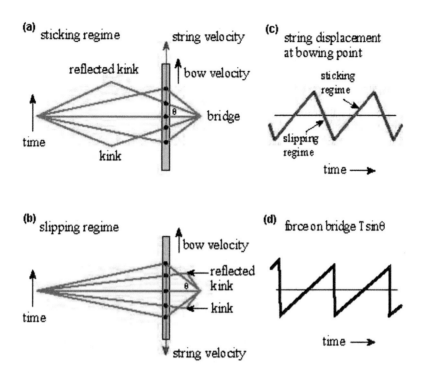

Figure 26 Dynamics of the Bow and Strings

Although the sliding friction is relatively small in the slipping regime, energy is continuously transferred from the strings to the vibrational modes of the instrument at the bridge. Each time the kink reflects back from the bridge and passes underneath the bow, the bow has to replace the lost energy. It therefore exerts a short impulse on the string so that it moves again at the same velocity as the bow.

This process is known as the 'slip-stick' mechanism of string excitation and relies on the fact that sliding friction is much smaller than sticking friction (Figure 26c). The Helmholtz wave generates a transverse force Tsinθ on the bridge, where θ is the angle of the string at the bridge. This force increases linearly with time, but its amplitude reverses suddenly each time the kink is reflected at the bridge, producing a sawtooth waveform (Figure 26d). The detailed physics of the way the bow excites a string has been extensively studied by J. McIntyre and J. Woodhouse at Cambridge University, who have made a number of important theoretical and experimental contributions to violin acoustics in recent years.

It is important to recognise that the Helmholtz wave is a free mode of vibration of the string. The player has to apply just the right amount of pressure to excite and maintain the waveform without destroying it. The lack of such skill is one of the main reasons why the sound produced by a beginner is so excruciating. Conversely, the intensity, quality and subtlety of sound produced by great violinists is mainly due to the fact that they can control the Helmholtz waveform with the bow. The quality of sound produced by any violin therefore depends as much on the bowing skill of the violinist as on the physical construction of the instrument. One of the reasons that the great Cremonese violins sound so wonderful is because we hear them played by the world's greatest players.

The Transformation of String Vibrations to Sound

The sawtooth force that is generated on the top of the bridge by a bowed string is the input signal that forces the violin to vibrate and radiate sound (Figure 27) – rather like the electrical input to a loudspeaker, albeit with a much more complicated frequency response. The input sawtooth waveform has a rich harmonic content, consisting of numerous Fourier components. (Jean-Baptste Joseph Fourier – was a French mathematician who devised a mathematical proof, which showed that any waveform can be de-composed into a summation of all the individual sinusoidal waveform harmonics contained in the waveshape).

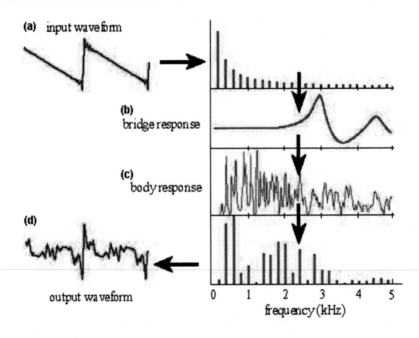

Figure 27 From Bowed Sawtooth Input at the Bridge to Melodic Output

Since the violin is a linear system, the same Fourier components or 'partials' (or overtones as Grant described them), appear in the output of the violin. The amplitude of each partial in the radiated sound is determined by the response of the instrument at that particular frequency. This is largely determined by the mechanical resonances of the bridge and by the body of the instrument. These resonances are illustrated schematically in Figure 26, where typical responses have been mathematically modelled to simulate their influence on the sound produced.

The Importance of the Bridge and the Transfer of Vibrations

At low frequencies, the bridge simply acts as a mechanical lever, since the response is independent of frequency. However, between 2.5 and 3 kHz the bowing action excites a strong resonance in the bridge, with the top rocking about its narrowed waist section. This boosts the intensity of any partials in this frequency range, where the ear is most sensitive, and gives greater brightness and carrying power to the sound. Another resonance occurs at about 4.5 kHz in which the bridge bounces up and down on its two feet. Between these two resonances there is a strong dip in the transfer of force to the body. Thankfully this dip decreases the amplitude of the partials at these frequencies, which the ear associates with an unpleasant shrillness in musical quality.

The sinusoidal force exerted by the bridge on the top plate produces an acoustic output that can be modelled mathematically. The output increases dramatically whenever the exciting frequency coincides with one of the many vibrational modes of the instrument. Indeed, the violin is rather like a loudspeaker with a highly non-uniform frequency response that peaks every time a resonance is excited. The modelled response is very similar to many recorded examples made on real instruments.

In practice, quite small changes in the arching, thickness and mass of the individual plates can result in big changes in the resonant frequencies of the violin, which is why no two instruments ever sound exactly alike. The multi-resonant response leads to dramatic variations in the amplitudes of individual partials for any note played on the violin.

Such factors must have unconsciously guided the radical redesign of the bridge in the 19th century. Violinists often place an additional mass (the 'mute') on top of the bridge, effectively lowering the frequency of the bridge resonances. This results in a much quieter and 'warmer' sound that players often use as a special effect. It is therefore surprising that so few players – or even violin makers – recognise the major importance of the bridge in determining the overall tone quality of an instrument. (Given the variety and number of different bridge pieces found in Grant's workshop archive, Figure 24, then perhaps he did).

One of the reasons for the excellent tone of the very best violins is the attention that top players give to the violin set-up – rather like the way in which a car engine is tuned to obtain the best performance. Violinists will, for example, carefully adjust the bridge to suit a particular instrument, or even select a different bridge altogether. The sound quality of many modern violins could undoubtedly be improved by taking just as much care in selecting and adjusting the bridge.

The transfer of energy from the vibrating string to the acoustically radiating structural modes is clearly essential for the instrument to produce any sound. However, this coupling must not be too strong, otherwise the instrument becomes difficult to play and the violinist has to work hard to maintain the Helmholtz wave. Indeed, a complete breakdown can occur when a string resonance coincides with a particularly strongly coupled and lightly damped structural resonance.

When this happens, the sound suddenly changes from a smooth tone to a quasi-periodic, uncontrollable, grunting sound – the 'wolf-note'. Players minimise this problem by wedging a duster against the top plate to dampen the vibrational modes, or by placing a resonating mass, the 'wolf-note adjuster', on one of the strings on the far side of the bridge. However, this only moves the wolf-note to a note that is not played as often, rather than eliminating it entirely.

The Helmholtz motion of the string and the wolf-note problem were extensively studied by the Indian physicist Chandrasekhara Raman in the early years of the 20th century. His results were published in a series of elegant theoretical and experimental papers soon after he founded the Indian Academy of Sciences and before the work on optics that earned him the Nobel Prize for Physics in 1930.

Tonal Quality, Resonances, and Instrument Design

The existence of so many resonances at almost random frequencies means that there is simply no such thing as a 'typical' waveform or spectrum for the sound from a violin. Indeed, there is just as much variation between the individual notes on a single instrument as there is between the same note played on different instruments. This implies that the perceived tone of a violin must be related to the overall design of the instrument, rather than to the frequencies of particular resonances on an instrument.

Is measured response a reliable guide to quality? Does it Help

An interesting attempt to look for such global properties was made at the turn of the century by the violin maker Heinrich Dunnwald in Germany. He measured the acoustic output of 10 Italian violins, 10 fine modern copies and 10 factory-made violins, all of which were excited by an electromagnetic driver on one side of the bridge (Figure 28). Between 400 and 600 Hz, the factory-made violins were found – surprisingly – to be closer to the Italian instruments than the modern copies. At frequencies above 1,000 Hz, however, the factory-made instruments had a rather weak response, in contrast to the over-strong response of the modern violins, which may contribute to a certain shrillness in their quality.

In practice it is extremely difficult to distinguish between a particularly fine Stradivarius instrument and an indifferent modern copy on the basis of the measured response alone. The ear is a supreme detection device and the brain is a far more sophisticated analyser of complex sounds than any system yet developed to assess musical quality.

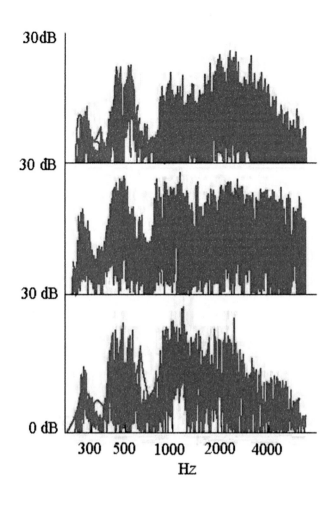

Figure 28 Typical acoustic output response of each of the three

different types of instruments tested

(Italian, fine modern copies, and factory made)

Although such measurements give the frequencies of important acoustic resonances, they tell us nothing about the way a violin actually vibrates. A powerful technique for investigating such vibrations is called "time-averaged interference holography". Bernard Richardson, a physicist at Cardiff University in the UK, has made a number of such studies on the guitar and violin. Some particularly beautiful examples for the guitar are shown in Figure 9. Unfortunately, it is not easy to obtain similar high-quality images for the violin because it is smaller, the vibrations of the surface are smaller, and the surfaces of the violin are more curved and less reflective than those of the guitar.

Another powerful approach is modal analysis: A violin is lightly struck with a calibrated hammer at several positions and the transient response at various points is measured with a very light accelerometer. These responses are then analysed by computer to give the resonant frequencies and structural modes of vibration of the whole instrument. This technique has been used to teach students about violin acoustics at the famous Mittenwald

School of Violin Making in Germany and by Ken Marshall in the US. Marshall has also shown that the way the violin is held has little effect on its resonant response.

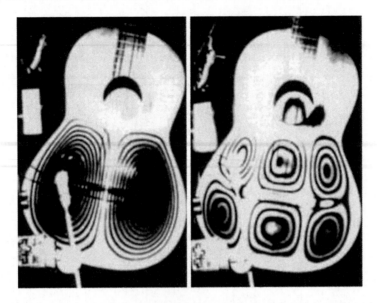

Figure 29 Interference Holography Pattern Illustrating Resonant

Vibrations Produced by a Guitar

Similar information can be obtained by finite-element analysis: the violin is modelled as a set of masses that are connected by springs, which makes it relatively straightforward to evaluate the resonant modes and associated vibrations of the whole structure. Various physical parameters of the materials used to make the violin can also be incorporated in the calculations. It is then possible to construct a virtual violin and to predict all its vibrational and acoustic properties. This might be the first step towards designing a violin with a specified response and hence tonal quality – once we know how to define 'quality' in a measurable way.

Is the use of vibrato an essential technical technique?

The strongly peaked frequency response of the violin has a dramatic influence on the sound produced when 'vibrato' is used. In this playing technique, the finger stopping the string is cyclically rocked backwards and forwards, periodically changing the pitch of the note. Because the response has such strong peaks and troughs, any change in pitch also produces cyclic variations in the overall amplitude, waveform and spectral content of the sound (Figure. 10).

The use of vibrato is very common nowadays because it captures and holds the attention of the listener, enabling the solo violin to be heard even when accompanied by a large orchestra. It would have been considered far less important when Stradivari was alive because vibrato was used only for special theatrical effects and the violin was expected to blend in with other instruments. Vibrato adds a certain 'lustre' and interest to the quality of sound produced because the ear is particularly sensitive to changes in the waveform. This in turn can result in the players subjective assessment of the sound as bringing 'life and vibrancy' to the sound.

To achieve such large changes in the frequency response of the violin, the individual resonances of the instrument have to be strongly peaked, which requires high-quality wood with low internal damping. Unfortunately, wood can absorb water, which increases the damping: This explains why violinists often notice that the responsiveness of an instrument, which includes the ability to control the sound quality using vibrato, changes with temperature and humidity.

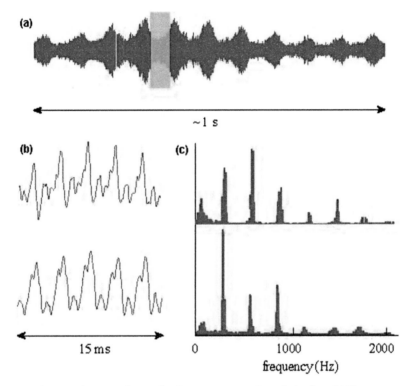

Figure 30 Strongly Peaked Resonances Result in Good Vibrato

Conclusion

Maybe there is an essential aspect of violin quality that we are still failing to recognise. Many violinists say they can distinguish an instrument with a fine 'Italian Cremonese sound' from one with, say, a more 'French' tone, such as a Vuillaume violin. But we still do not know how to characterize such properties in meaningful physical terms.

References:

1. McIntyre, M. E. and Woodhouse, J., :'On the Fundamentals of Bowed String Dynamics'. 1981, Acustica, 42 93.
2. Kerr, M. F., :'An account of violin Geometry'. Private Publication.
3. Gough, G., :'Science and the Stradivarius'. Pub. Physics World, 01 Apr. 2000'.

4. Fletcher, N. and H., Rossing, T. D., :'The Physics of Musical Instruments'. 2nd Edn., Springer, New York.

5. Hutchins, C. M. and Benade, V., :'Research Papers in Violin Acoustics'. 197593, vols 1 and 2, 1997. The Acoustical Society of America, New York.

6. Cremer, L., :'The Physics of the Violin'. MIT Press, (essential physics of violin acoustics).

References, Acknowledgements, and Further General Reading

References:

Inverness Museum & Art Gallery (IMAG)

Highlife Highland Archive Services, Inverness (www.ambaile.org.uk)

Physics World, Published by the Institute of Physics

'A data-driven approach to violin making'. Scientific reports. Open Access.

Inverness Remembered, Inverness Courier, Vol.1V, Printed by Inverness Courier

Acknowledgements:

Michael Kerr, Great Grandson of Alexander 'Battan' Grant

Donald Fraser at Donald Morison Ironmonger, Station Road, Beauly

Quest for the Round Fiddle of Strathspey, Archie Fisher, Radio Scotland, 18/12/1976

Inverness Local History Forum– promotion of Lecture on Grant, (S. Gair)

Inverness Townscape Heritage Project – promotion of Lecture on Grant, (S. Gair)

General - Further Reading:

'Fine and Far Off'. Salmon Fishing Methods in Practice, By Jock Scott, Pub. Seeley Service & C0. Ltd. 196 Shaftesbury Avenue, London. (Pub. Around 1942/43)

'Old Inverness in Pictures', Inverness Field Club; Paul Harris Publishing, 1978

'The Banks of the Ness', Mairi A MacDonald; Paul Harris Publishing, 1982

Media References

Pall Mall Gazette Dec 1896:

Details of fly casting demonstration at Kingston-upon- Thames. Editors of "The Field" and "Land & Water" present.

Highland News 6 – 6 – 1908:

Contents unknown.

Daily Record 31 – 3 – 1936:

Left school at 8...when 10 refused fiddle lessons because tutor's fiddle had poor tone...in turn ploughman, shepherd, draper, forester, grocer, butcher, gamekeeper, fisherman and fishing tackle merchant in Inverness...retired 30 years ago...40 years leader of Inverness Strathspey and Reel Society.
